Learning Pixelmator

Enhance your photos effectively and unleash
the artist inside, with Pixelmator

Mark Stagi

PUBLISHING

BIRMINGHAM - MUMBAI

Learning Pixelmator

First published: April 2013

Production Reference: 1040413

Published by Packt Publishing Ltd.
Livery Place
35 Livery Street
Birmingham B3 2PB, UK.

ISBN 978-1-84969-468-1

www.packtpub.com

Cover Image by Artie Ng (artherng@yahoo.com.au)

Credits

Author
Mark Stagi

Reviewer
Paul Kercal

Acquisition Editor
Edward Gordon

Lead Technical Editor
Meeta Rajani

Technical Editors
Dennis John

Saijul Shah

Copy Editors
Alfida Paiva

Aditya Nair

Laxmi Subramanian

Brandt D'Mello

Project Coordinator
Siddhant Shetty

Proofreader
Samantha Lyon

Indexer
Tejal R. Soni

Production Coordinator
Conidon Miranda

Cover Work
Conidon Miranda

About the Author

Mark Stagi has been passionate about photography since catching the photo bug as a child. Mark got fully hooked in the darkroom while in high school when watching the magic of a print appear. In college, Mark continued his studies of Photography and Fine Art with a degree in the Arts and an emphasis on Photography. Right after college, Mark started his own wedding photography business focusing on Fine Art Wedding photography. Mark's wedding business all started with his passion to create fresh and fun wedding images that reflect each bride's unique day.

Growing up in the Silicon Valley, Mark has always had as much of a passion for technology as he has with the arts. As the photo industry started to move over into the digital world, Mark has been at the forefront of mastering the digital tools that photographers need to create art.

Mark's passion for photography has also led him to lead photography workshops and run a photography website http://www.digitalphotobuzz.com, where he shares his passion and love for photography with Shooting Tips, Online Tutorials, and other photography news and info.

Mark has written a few other mini books that are currently available as apps for the iPad, including *Portrait Photography 101 – Learn to take better portraits*, *Wedding Photography – A guide to better wedding photos*, *Baby Photography*, among others.

First off I would like to give thanks to God for giving me the passion to create, the direction to follow my dreams, and the artistic gifts he has given me. I am continually thankful and blessed to have breath each and every day.

This book would also not have been possible without my other half, my wonderful wife Lisa. She has always encouraged me to follow my dreams, provides continual support to our family, and allows me the time and focus to fulfill my purpose. She is my best friend, the best mother, and I am thankful for her huge support.

I also have to mention our two amazing children that bring a smile to my face each and every day. No matter how much busy work or things life throws at me, they keep me smiling.

About the Reviewer

Paul Kercal is a next generation digital graphics educator, a youth worker, a tablet and desktop artist, and a writer. For the past 15 years, he's worked firstly as the manager of a thriving youth arts center, and for the past decade, as a college arts teacher for a successful and thriving digital graphics course. He's written everything from teenage adventure fiction (the *Dr Sylver* series, *Messenger*) to art workbooks and how-to guides (*Stylus t. Frog and the Weapons of Mass Construction* being the most recent).

When creating artwork, he's extremely fond of Pixelmator (of course), Photoshop, Expression, and a whole host of tablet art apps including Brushes V2, Ideas, ArtRage, ProCreate, and more.

I'd like to thank everyone who have made this year so exciting in the digital and real world! It's never been a more exciting time to be a digital artist, so the makers and creators of the apps and programs that allow dreams to be drawn, thank you! Also to wifey, as I should offer thanks always.

www.PacktPub.com

Support files, eBooks, discount offers and more

You might want to visit www.PacktPub.com for support files and downloads related to your book.

Did you know that Packt offers eBook versions of every book published, with PDF and ePub files available? You can upgrade to the eBook version at www.PacktPub.com and as a print book customer, you are entitled to a discount on the eBook copy. Get in touch with us at service@packtpub.com for more details.

At www.PacktPub.com, you can also read a collection of free technical articles, sign up for a range of free newsletters and receive exclusive discounts and offers on Packt books and eBooks.

http://PacktLib.PacktPub.com

Do you need instant solutions to your IT questions? PacktLib is Packt's online digital book library. Here, you can access, read and search across Packt's entire library of books.

Why Subscribe?
- Fully searchable across every book published by Packt
- Copy and paste, print and bookmark content
- On demand and accessible via web browser

Free Access for Packt account holders

If you have an account with Packt at www.PacktPub.com, you can use this to access PacktLib today and view nine entirely free books. Simply use your login credentials for immediate access.

Table of Contents

Preface

Pixelmator is one of those applications that has such a beautiful and sleek look to it. At first glance it can seem like a very simple application, but as with many things in life, looks can be deceiving and Pixelmator is a great example of a well-designed application that has a lot of power underneath the interface, and helps to give digital artists and photographers the tools that we need to unleash the creative process inside. Pixelmator gives us many of the strong tools that other applications have at a fraction of the cost, making it a must-have application for photographers at any level out there.

What this book covers

Chapter 1, Basic Photo Corrections gives an understanding of the tools available in Pixelmator and how to get started with importing your images. We will also cover some basic photo corrections.

Chapter 2, Using Selection Tools discusses one of the fundamental tools in image editing used to precisely select parts of an image. Here you will learn how to use the many selection tools available in Pixelmator.

Chapter 3, All About Layers discusses layers that will allow us to get creative with multi-image layouts. We will walk through all of the ways you can adjust layers to creatively edit your images.

Chapter 4, Using the Effects Browser Tools discusses a wealth of tools to apply image effects to your projects. We will walk through all of the available effects to get your creativity flowing.

Chapter 5, More Creative Photo Corrections will make you learn about some of the more advanced image editing tools such as the clone stamp tool, and using shapes, text, and gradients to embellish your images.

Chapter 6, Advanced Pixelmator Techniques will walk through some real-world tutorials with some advanced image-editing techniques to bring everything we have learned in the book together.

What you need for this book

This book covers Pixelmator version 2.1.4 and a creative attitude is all that's needed for this book to learn the application.

Who this book is for

This book is for any digital artist, photographer, or photo enthusiast looking to unleash their full creativity by learning how to edit their images in Pixelmator.

Conventions

In this book, you will find a number of styles of text that distinguish between different kinds of information. Here are some examples of these styles, and an explanation of their meaning.

New terms and **important words** are shown in bold. Words that you see on the screen, in menus or dialog boxes for example, appear in the text like this: " First, if the **Effects Browser** panel isn't open you can click **View** | **Show Effects**".

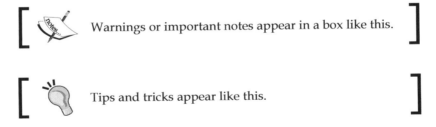

Warnings or important notes appear in a box like this.

Tips and tricks appear like this.

Reader feedback

Feedback from our readers is always welcome. Let us know what you think about this book—what you liked or may have disliked. Reader feedback is important for us to develop titles that you really get the most out of.

To send us general feedback, simply send an e-mail to feedback@packtpub.com, and mention the book title through the subject of your message.

If there is a topic that you have expertise in and you are interested in either writing or contributing to a book, see our author guide on www.packtpub.com/authors.

Customer support

Now that you are the proud owner of a Packt book, we have a number of things to help you to get the most from your purchase.

Errata

Although we have taken every care to ensure the accuracy of our content, mistakes do happen. If you find a mistake in one of our books—maybe a mistake in the text or the code—we would be grateful if you would report this to us. By doing so, you can save other readers from frustration and help us improve subsequent versions of this book. If you find any errata, please report them by visiting http://www.packtpub.com/support, selecting your book, clicking on the **errata submission form** link, and entering the details of your errata. Once your errata are verified, your submission will be accepted and the errata will be uploaded to our website, or added to any list of existing errata, under the Errata section of that title.

Piracy

Piracy of copyright material on the Internet is an ongoing problem across all media. At Packt, we take the protection of our copyright and licenses very seriously. If you come across any illegal copies of our works, in any form, on the Internet, please provide us with the location address or website name immediately so that we can pursue a remedy.

Please contact us at copyright@packtpub.com with a link to the suspected pirated material.

We appreciate your help in protecting our authors, and our ability to bring you valuable content.

Questions

You can contact us at questions@packtpub.com if you are having a problem with any aspect of the book, and we will do our best to address it.

1
Basic Photo Corrections

Pixelmator has many tools that will give you very advanced ways to edit your photos, no matter what your level of photography. It's one of those applications that has a beautiful and sleek look to it. At first glance it can seem like a very simple application. Just like many things in life, looks can be deceiving, and Pixelmator is a great example of a well-designed application that has a lot of power underneath the interface and helps to give digital artists and photographers the tools they need to unleash their creative process. Pixelmator gives us many of the strong tools that other applications have at a fraction of the cost, making it a must-have app for photographers at any level out there.

With Pixelmator, you can unleash the creative artist inside and enhance your photos.

Installing Pixelmator

Pixelmator is a Mac-only app and can be purchased through the Mac App store.

Purchasing and installing Pixelmator is very easy through the Mac App store. Just launch the app store on your mac and search for `Pixelmator`, click on purchase and sign in with your iTunes credentials to compete the purchase and installation of the app. You can also download a 30-day free trial from their website at `http://www.pixelmator.com/try/`.

Starting with a new blank image and importing files

To get started, we will use a blank document and walk through the important settings to get your document started on the right foot. When you open Pixelmator, go to the **File | New** menu option (or click *Command + N*). Here you will be greeted with a simple dialog box to set your image dimensions. The size and resolution you set for the final image is very important, so make sure to select the largest size you think you might possibly use. Say you are creating a collage of images for a poster that you think you are going to print with a 11 x 14 size. After working on it for hours you create a final masterpiece and love it so much you want to print it with a size of 30 x 40. Well, sorry to say, but once you scale something up after editing you will lose a ton of quality in the image and have a pretty poor quality 30 x 40 poster. So always remember to set the size of the image from the very start to as large as you might possibly want to print; you can always size down later but cannot size up.

When choosing the size and resolution you will be able to enter in anything freeform or click on the **Preset** dropdown at the top to choose from many popular sizes such as **1280 x 800** or an **8 x 10** inch option for printing. The resolution is just as important as the physical size and really depends on what type of medium you are going to have as your final outcome. If you are only creating something to view on a computer, 72 pixels/inch (PPI) is all you need, that's the max that a screen can display. However, if you are going to print an image, then you should set the resolution higher; 300 PPI should be perfect.

 When you go to print a digital image, the pixels are converted to dots. This is where you hear the term **dots per inch** (**DPI**). Because these dots have spaces between them, 300 PPI isn't equal to 300 DPI. If your image is 300 PPI, pixels become roughly 150 DPI. In the printing world, 150 DPI is the standard for printing photographic quality images.

One very useful feature is the ability to create your own presets. If you use a specific custom size over and over again, it will save time to create a custom preset with this size. To do this, first set the width, height, and resolution, and then click on the gear icon on the bottom-left corner of the dialog box. Here you will see a **Save Preset As...** option as shown in the following screenshot:

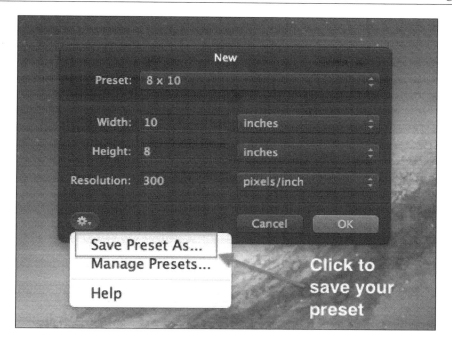

Click on this and name your preset to save this for future use. Presets are also grouped by a few predefined types, namely, **Screen**, **Web**, **Photo**, **Print**, and **Other**, which help in organizing your list.

 Using presets and keyboard shortcuts will always save a lot of time in the long run. As you work, remember to save the most common tasks you do as presets if possible.

Once you have the size and resolution set up, you will see a blank canvas waiting for you to start getting creative with. There are a few ways you can add images to this blank canvas. The easiest way is just a simple drag-and-drop. Simply open up a new Finder window on your computer and navigate to the image you would like to add to the canvas. Then drag-and-drop the photo to place it. It might not be sized exactly how you want it to be, but we will be able to adjust this at any time; we will cover how to resize images later on in this chapter.

Here you can see just how easy it is to drag-and-drop a new image into an existing Pixelmator project:

You can also use the **Import** menu button in the **File** menu to add images, if you have your camera or a card reader connected to the computer. This will bring up an **Import** dialog box which will give you the ability to selectively import certain images by *Command* + clicking on specific images or clicking on the **Import All** button.

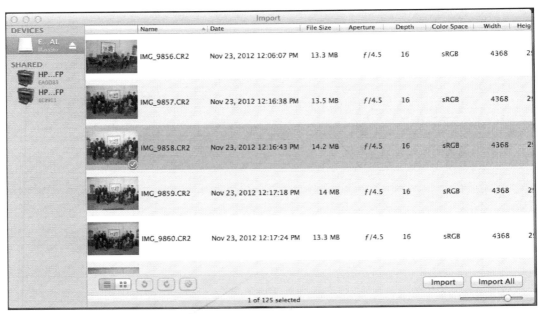

Another way to add images to your canvas is to use the *Command + 6* key combination and open up the **Photo Browser**. Here you will have the ability to browse through your **iPhoto** library or the **Pictures** folder. If you have a huge folder of files, just use the search at the bottom of the **Photo Browser** to perform a search.

Once you have dragged a photo into the canvas, just use the move tool to move it to the area you would like.

Resolution and image size

As we talked about at the start of this chapter, your image size and resolution is very important. Let's take a few minutes before moving on to talk a little more about what image resolution really is. All digital images are made up of **pixels**, which are tiny squares filled with a solid color. When you have many of these tiny squares filled with shades of different colors, you get the appearance of a smooth image. Photos are taken at different resolutions depending on the camera and settings. In today's market, many **digital single-lens reflex** (DSLR) cameras can have a resolution up to 5616 × 3744 pixels.

Within Pixelmator, you can adjust the resolution and image size by going to the **Image | Image Size**. Here, you will be able to change the height and width of the image and have it set as either **pixels, percent, inches, cm, mm**, or **points**. There are a few things that you want to make sure to keep in mind when changing the image size. First, unless you want to distort the image you will want to keep the checkbox for scale proportionally checked. This will ensure that any change you make to the height of the image will proportionally change the width as well and vice versa, so there is no distortion in the image.

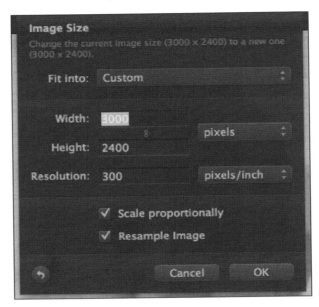

Another thing to keep in mind is that you normally don't want to size things up too much. Say you have an image that is 3000 x 2000 pixels and you want to increase the width to 4000 pixels. You will have to make sure that the **Resample Image** option is checked at the bottom of the **Image Size** menu. But how does Pixelmator add 1000 pixels to the width of the image? The key is **resampling**, which basically means that the program is going to add new pixels to the image by guessing, based on the surrounding colors. Since the program is basically guessing (although it is a very smart guess) on what types of pixels to add, you get a loss of sharpness, so as a general guideline it's not recommended to go up in size too much.

Customizing the workspace

Since all photographers will use Pixelmator for different uses, you will want to get the workspace configured to match the way you like to work and the tools that you really need the most. Aside from the main image window, there are a few other windows that you will usually want to make visible, such as the **Tools, Layers, Effects Browser, Brushes, Gradients, Photo Browser, Fonts,** and **Colors**. You will always want some of these windows (such as the **Tools** window) open, while others (such as **Fonts)** you might only need from time to time. You can always turn on/off menu items from the **View** menu. The windows can be positioned anywhere on your screen as per your needs by clicking-and-dragging the top section of the window.

You can also use the arrows icon on the top-right corner of your image window to enter a full-screen mode, or go to **View | Enter Full Screen** (keyboard shortcut is *Control + Command + F*). This will expand the image and make it full screen to clear out any distractions that you might have running on in your desktop.

Overview of the layout and tool panes

The overall layout of Pixelmator is composed of your main image window and many other toolbars that can be shown/hidden depending on your workflow. Let's first start with the main window where your image is located. You can always use the *Command + 0* keyboard shortcut to fit the photo on the screen or use *Command + –/+* to zoom in/out of the image. You can also zoom to the actual size of the image by using the shortcut *Alt + Command + 0*. If you want to see what zoom level you are currently at, just click on the **Magnify** icon on the tool bar and you will see the percent zoom indicated at the top-middle of the window.

Rulers

The main image window has many options you can customize. The most common thing that you might want to turn on is to show the rulers on the x and y axis. This will show you rulers spanning the top and left-hand side of the window. The measurement that the ruler is shown in will be set in pixels by default, but can be edited by going to **Pixelmator | Preferences | Rulers**. Here set the default ruler units to **Pixels, Inches, Centimeters, Millimeters, Points, Picas,** or **Percent**. You can use the *Command + R* shortcut to toggle on and off with the ruler view.

Turning on or off the **Rulers** option (as well as any other options for the main image window) can all be accessed in the **View** menu or with keyboard shortcuts.

Another option that can be helpful is the grid view. You can show a grid overlay on the image, which can be very helpful when alighting items. The keyboard shortcut to show the grid view is *Alt + Command + '*. The following screenshot is an example of what the default grid lines look like over an image:

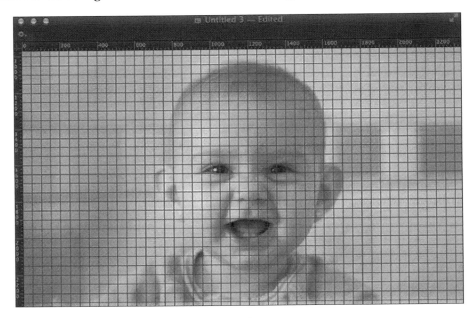

The gridlines can also be customized in the main preferences screen by navigating to **Pixelmator | Preferences | Rulers**. You are able to set the color of the gridlines and the number of pixels between the gridlines and subdivisions.

Guides

Guides are another very helpful viewing option, especially when you are trying to create a page layout or a collage with many images and need to alight them in a certain way. Guides are easy to create, but first make sure you have them turned on by going to **View | Guides | Show Guides** or using the keyboard shortcut *Alt + Command + ;*. Once you have the view turned on, you can add as many guides as you need by simply clicking and holding down the mouse then dragging from the left-hand side or top edge where the ruler is. As you drag your mouse along, you will see a counter showing exactly where you are on the ruler and the blue guide line. In the following screenshot, you can see how the guidelines show up on your canvas:

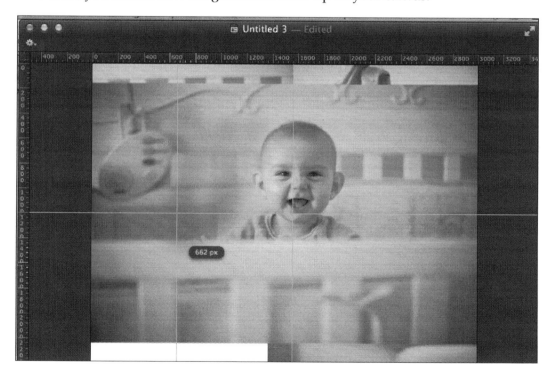

Release the mouse to place the guide. If you ever need to move a guide, you can always move it later. Moving a guideline is easy, move your mouse over the guideline and then click-and-drag to reposition it anywhere on the canvas.

There are also a few other settings for guides that can be very helpful. These are all located at **View | Guides**. The first option in this menu is called **Show Guides at Object Center**. This is very helpful when trying to position an image in the very center of the document. Once it's turned on and you are going to move any layer, you will see a blue guideline appear when the center of that layer is in the center of the overall canvas or the center of any other layers on the canvas.

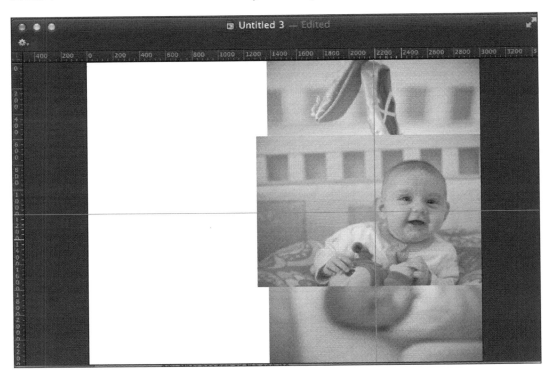

You can also turn on the option to **Show Guides at Object Edges**.

The **Guides** menu has two additional items you can turn on. The first option is **Show relative spacing**. This option only works when you have three or more objects that are lined up on the canvas. Say you are trying to line up three images to be printed in one large horizontal photo and you want equal spacing between the three photos. When you move one image so that it's equal in distance compared to the two other images, a purple object spacing guide will show you the distance between the images in the current ruler unit that you are using.

In this image, you can see that the images have an equal spacing in between them by using the relative spacing option:

The last option in the guide's menu is to show relative sizing. When this option is checked and you are transforming the size of an image, you will see a purple sizing guide appear when the height and width are the same for both images.

In the following screenshot, you can see that the two images on the left-hand side of the canvas are of the same exact size:

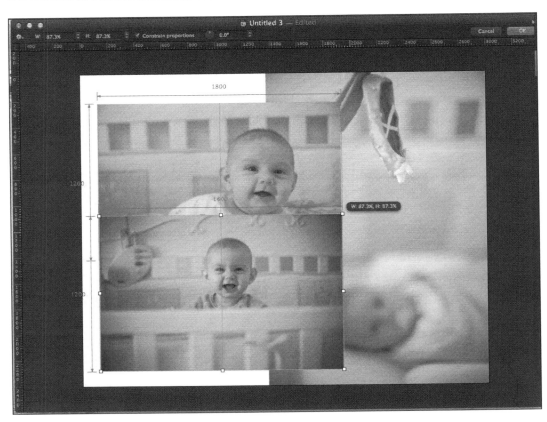

Using rulers, grids, and guides will help you save a lot of time getting different layers positioned just right and also help you edit layouts with precision. You can also change the default color of the guides and object spacing by navigating to **Pixelmator | Preferences** and accessing the **Ruler Preferences** menu to choose your own color from the color picker instead of the default blue and purple that Pixelmator sets.

Tool options and info bar

One very important menu is at the very top of the image window on the left-hand side. Here you will see a gear icon that is clickable and shows additional options for the tool that you have selected. I'll refer to this menu throughout the book as the **tool settings menu**. With this tool settings menu, you will see context-sensitive settings based on the tool that you are currently using. Whenever you first use a tool, it's a good practice to view what options are available for that tool under this settings menu.

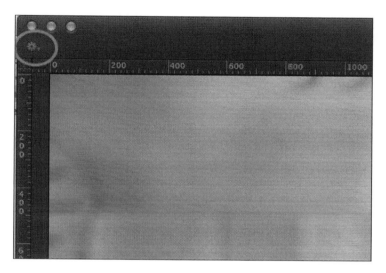

Also, on the top of the image window you will have a list of other options spanning across the top. These options will be different depending on the tool you are currently in. For example, if you are using the crop tool, you will see options to constrain the proportions of the crop; and if you are using the Paint Bucket tool, you will see options to pick your color and also the blend options for the tool.

You can turn this on and off by navigating to the **Show/Hide Tool** options in the **View** menu.

There is also an info bar that is shown right below the tools options at the top of the main image window. This can also be turned on/off in the **Show/Hide Info Bar** options in the **View** menu. Once you turn this bar on, you can also customize what shows up on this by *Control* + clicking in this area to bring up a list of options you can turn on or off.

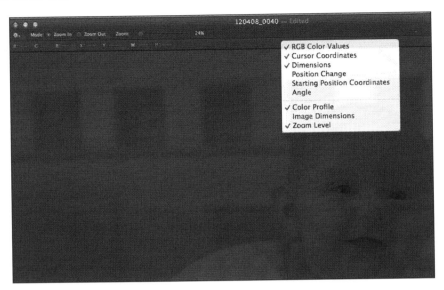

The Tools bar

The **Tools** pane is one of the most important menu bars that you constantly use. Here you will see 28 different tools that Pixelmator has. We will cover the details on many of these tools later on in this book. To add or remove tools from this menu, navigate to **Pixelmator | Preferences | Tools**. From here you can drag additional tools into the toolbar or drag any of them you don't need outside of the toolbar.

Before we get into using some of the tools and making adjustments, one of the most commonly used keyboard shortcuts that you will use is the *Command* + *Z* shortcut to undo your last action. You can continue using the *Command* + *Z* shortcut to go back as many steps as you need. There is also a redo shortcut at *Shift* + *Command* + *Z*.

Using some of the common tools for image editing

This section will cover common tools used for editing and enhancing images.

Adjusting color

One of the most common adjustments that need to be made with digital photos is fixing the color balance. You might have taken a photo outside and forgot to change the white balance from **Tungsten** earlier in the day to **Daylight**. Or you left the white balance on auto and the skin tones are just a little off. Pixelmator has some easy color effects to fix any color balance issues or to make artistic adjustments such as changing a photo to black and white. All of the color adjustments will be done in the **Effects** browser. If you don't have this window visible, it can be found on the menu under **View | Show Effects**. Once this window is up, select the **Color Adjustments** option from the drop-down menu at the top.

Before we start making adjustments to the image's color, it's always a good idea to duplicate the layer you are working on. This way, if you ever need to easily go back to the original, you can delete the new layer you are working on and always have the main layer still intact. To do this, navigate to **Edit | Duplicate**. To make adjustments to the overall color of the image, double-click on the **Color Balance** button. This will open up sliders to change the **Cyan/Red**, **Magenta/Green**, or **Yellow/Blue** color balance within the **Shadows**, **Midtones**, and **Highlight** areas.

Let's start with this image that came straight out of the camera. This image was taken inside and the white balance of the camera was set to **Tungsten**. Although it was inside, there was hardly any indoor light and the main light on the scene was from a window that has some great sunlight coming in. The white balance should have been set to *Daylight* or *Cloudy* on the camera to get the color balance closer to reality. Since the color of the image is very cold, we need to warm it up a bit.

Let's walk through the steps to correct this:

1. First, start with the **Midtones** and start to adjust the colors one by one. You can see that this original image has too much green and blue colors in it. So I'll start by moving the **Magenta/Green** slider over to the magenta side to add more magenta to the midtones of the image.

2. Next, move over to the **Yellow/Blue** slider and start to add some yellow shade to the image.

3. You can also see that there is a slight cyan tint so move the **Cyan/Red** slider over to the red side slightly to add just a little bit of red shade to the image.

4. Next, proceed to make the needed color changes to the **Shadows** and **Highlights** until you get the perfect image.

Also remember that while there is technically a correct color, you should always color-balance things to fit your exact style of photography. I love to have many of my portraits contain an extra warmth to the image and while I might add more yellow to a portrait than other people would, it fits my creative vision and style for the shot. Here is what the final color of the flowers look like, much more natural!

Straightening and cropping

Cropping can be the key that separates a great image from a decent image. Although as artists we should always try to capture the perfect image in camera while taking the photo, many times it just doesn't work out perfectly. The crop tool can quickly be accessed by using the keyboard shortcut of *C*.

Once you have the crop tool selected, click-and-drag on the image to make your crop selection. You can set the proportions of the crop to be constrained to a specific ratio or even be a freeform crop by selecting an option from the **Constrain** menu in the toolbar.

After you have drawn the initial selection on the image, you can refine the selection by moving your cursor to one of the four corners of the selection and using a click-and-drag action to move your selection. You can also rotate the image if you need to straighten a part of the photo. To straighten the image while cropping, move the cursor to just outside of the corners of the selection box; it will turn the cursor to show a 90-degree arrow. Now click-and-drag the image to rotate.

After you have the crop selection perfect and are ready to crop, you first have to select the crop mode. There are just two crop modes to choose from: **Hide** or **Delete**. The difference between the two is what happens to the part of the image you are cropping out. With **Delete** it's pretty straightforward, the image you are cropping out gets deleted. When choosing **Hide** however, it will crop the image but keep the part cropped out invisible so you can always move the image after it's cropped to bring back those cropped parts. This comes in handy if you need to alter the crop afterwards, since the data is still there, just select the move tool (keyboard shortcut M) and move the image around, anything outside of the frame will appear. After you select the crop mode either double-click within the cropped part or press the *Enter* key to finish cropping the image.

Red eye reduction

Another common issue with some flash photos is the infamous red eye. **Red eye** is caused when you have a flash very close to the axis of the camera lens. Because of the position of the flash the light reflects off the back of the persons eyeball and comes back out through the pupil, and since there is ample blood in the back of the eye, it shows through as red to the camera. In Pixelmator, you can fix red eye either automatically or manually. To have it automatically fix red eye, all you have to do is click on the red eye tool in your tool menu and then in the tool settings menu select **Auto Fix Red Eye**. Just like magic the red eye will be removed. As with many things, an automated process isn't perfect and will not always get the red eye out, so you might want to manually remove the red eye from the photo.

To manually remove the red eye, just perform the following steps:

1. Adjust the **Diameter** slider at the top to be approximately the size of the person's pupil.

2. Then click on the pupil and the red eye will be removed.

When removing red eye, first use the zoom tool to zoom in on the eye, so when you adjust the diameter you can select only the pupil that needs to be corrected.
You can always get a better selection when you are zoomed in nice and tight.

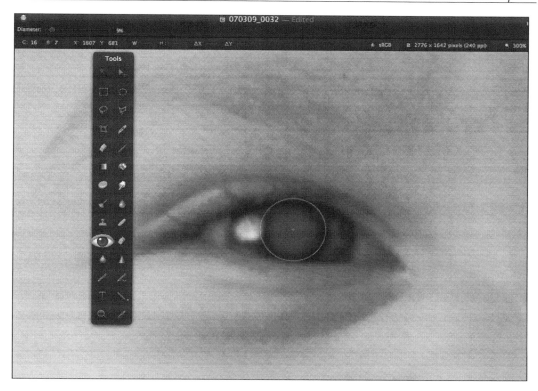

Dodge and burn

Dodging and burning is a term from the old days of printing in a darkroom. Back then, photographers had to use an enlarger to place a focused beam of light through a film negative to expose a light-sensitive piece of photo paper. When you wanted part of the image to be lighter, you would "dodge" that area by covering the light from hitting the sensitive photo paper. Alternatively, if you wanted part of the photo to be darker, you would "burn" parts of the photo by allowing light to only hit a certain part of the photo.

Dodging and burning in the digital realm is pretty much the same concept, you are going to be either adding or removing light from a scene. This can be done as follows:

1. We will start with the burn tool, which looks like a small orange flame in the tools menu.

2. Once you select the burn tool, you will want to click on the brush image that is on the top of the image window next to the tool settings menu.

3. When you click on this, it will open up a new pop-up window showing a list of brushes to pick. Having the right brush is essential to making a smooth burn on the image.

Before we get into how to choose the right brush, let's talk a little more about why you want to dodge or burn a photo. Normally, you will want to burn an area of a photo where you don't want people to focus their eye on. If you have a portrait and want people to focus directly on the person, you might want to burn in the edges of the photo so the readers eye is driven right to the main subject. It is natural reaction for someone who is looking at a photo to automatically have their eye first go to the lightest part of the image. The highlights really draw the user's attention, but many times we don't want them to focus on these highlights. You might have some bright areas around the edges of a portrait; however, you don't want the viewer to focus on the edge of the picture but instead to focus on your subject.

Example on dodging and burning

Now let's walk through an example on dodging and burning.

1. Start with a hard brush that has a 200-pixel diameter.

2. Next, set the exposure to be 65 percent. The exposure will control how much "light" will hit the photo so how dark it will be as you brush it on.

3. Do a couple of quick swipes back and forth over the top-left area of the photo. You will see when you go over the same area with the burn brush; it will get darker and darker with every pass. When you burn something in too much, it's pretty harsh and really is distracting.

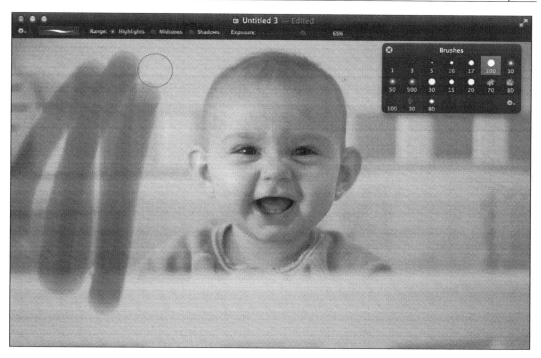

Instead of having these hard lines, let's change the brush up to a 500-pixel diameter brush and also one that has 0 hardness. The hardness controls the edge of the brush, so instead of having a hard line edge this will have a soft edge. The **Brushes** window menu can be accessed by using the keyboard shortcut *Command + 4*. This will give you a few preset brushes, but you can also customize these to create your own brushes. To open up the additional brush settings, first click on the gear icon on the bottom-right corner of the **Brushes** window and select **Show Brush Settings**.

Here you will see a wide range of options to customize your brush. You can set the size of the brush, hardness of the brush, as well as many other fine-tune adjustments such as the spacing and scatter. As you adjust the brush settings, you will see a preview brush stroke show up at the bottom of the **Brush** window.

When using the larger and softer brush, you will see that you get a much more natural and smooth transition from the dark areas you are painting into the other areas that you aren't changing.

Blur and sharpen tools

The blur and sharpen tools are similar, in a way, to the dodge and burn tools. These are tools that help you brush on certain effects of the photo and instead of making the image darker or lighter, you can make it more or less sharp. This also helps to guide the user's eye around the photo and is very important in having your photo tell a story. Just like the viewer's eye in a photo goes to the lightest part of the print, their eye also goes to the sharpest part of the print. So having certain parts be super sharp and others be soft will let you be a visual storyteller and guide the reader's eye throughout the photo.

To use the blur tool, click on the icon that looks like a water droplet in the tools menu. At the top of the image menu, you can adjust the strength of the blur and also click on the brush icon in order to customize the brush size, hardness, and other details. There are many different ways you can use the blur tool, but a common use is to smooth out skin. If you are using the tool to soften skin, you should select a brush that has a very low hardness so the blur effect fades into the rest of the skin in a very natural way. Brush the effect on to the areas you would like to blur. It's also a good idea to start with a lower strength in the blur options and paint the effect over and over to get the most natural look to the effect.

 When adjusting the size of any brush you can use the [and] keys to make your brush smaller/larger.

The sharpen tool works exactly in the same manner as the blur tool just giving you the opposite effect. You can click on the cone icon in the tools menu or use the keyboard shortcut of the *O* key. Sharpening can be important to guide the viewer's eye around your photo. You can give the eyes of a portrait a little sharpening to focus the viewers right into the eyes or sharpen parts of a landscape to give a certain part of the landscape more focus in the image.

Blurring and sharpening the image should be used to fine-tune your photography and help to tell the full artistic story of the shot.

Summary

We covered a lot of ground in this first chapter to give you a good foundation on Pixelmator. We learned how to get started with a blank canvas and how setting the right size is important at the beginning. We also walked through importing images on to a canvas and went over the layout of the canvas and tools. In the latter half of the chapter, we went over using some of the common tools for image editing.

Now that we have a good understanding on how to import your images into Pixelmator and perform some simple adjustments, we will move onto using the various selections tools in the next chapter.

2
Using Selection Tools

In this chapter we will cover what selections are and how to use selections in order to edit certain parts of your images.

Selections are a key to work with images in Pixelmator. Often, you are going to edit only certain parts of an image and don't want your effects to be applied to the entire image. Selecting the part of the image you want to edit might not be an easy task. As with most things in the real world, items aren't going to be a perfectly-shaped rectangle or circle, so making a selection can take a good amount of work and the right tools for the job. There are seven different selection tools and they are all located at the top of the **Tools** menu. I'll walk you through the advantages of each one of the tools and show you how to select objects quickly but also with precision. Before we talk about selecting, though, we will review a few tools that you will use to move and transform your images.

The Move tool

Before getting into the numerous ways that can be used to make selections, let's talk about a tool you will use alongside the selection tools. This tool is located in the same area as the selection tools and goes hand in hand with them. It's the move tool and is located in the top right of the **Tools** menu, or can be accessed by the keyboard shortcut *V*. This tool does just what it says; when you have a layer selected, it will move the layer so you can position the layer into a specific space. There are a few other options that the move tool has that are very useful. These all can be accessed under the gear icon on the top left of the image window when you are in the Move tool. These options include things such as rotating the image or flipping the photo horizontally or vertically.

When you have the move tool selected, hold down the *Alt* key then click-and-drag on a layer. This will create a copy of the layer.

Working with the Transform tool

The **Transform** tool is one of the most useful all-round tools when editing multiphoto layouts. Whenever you need to change the size of a layer, just go to **Transform** (the keyboard shortcut is *command + F*). When you are using the **Transform** tool, it will place handles on the corners and on the middle edge of the photo. Just click-and-drag these handles to make the photo larger/smaller. Also, if you move the cursor slightly outside of the handle, your cursor will change to a rotate cursor and you can click-and-drag to rotate the photo.

While you are using the **Transform** tool, the gear icon on the top left will change with some additional options. The default option is **Free Transform...**; this will let you scale the image up and down, but the three additional options below **Free Transform...** give you some additional creative control. The first is **Skew...**.

Skew

Here you will be able to drag out any corner of the image to extend that side of the image. In the following image, you can see that the top-right corner of the image has been stretched out:

Distort

You can also use the **Distort...** option to stretch out an image. This is similar to the **Skew...** option, but it differs in that it allows you to drag the corner in any direction. The **Skew...** option is limited to only moving out the corner vertically or horizontally, but not both.

Perspective

Finally you can use the **Perspective...** option. This allows you to create a 3D type perspective on the layer, making the top or bottom of the image wider so that it looks like the layer is coming off the page. Normally, the **Skew...**, **Distort...**, and **Perspective...** options aren't going to be used daily. For many of you, however, from time to time they do come in handy for creating a certain special effect.

Rotating and flipping

Another option you have in the **Move** menu is to rotate the layer. You can rotate the layer 180 degrees or 90 degrees to the right or left. Besides accessing these in the Move Tool settings menu, you can also get to these tools in the main **Edit** menu at the top of your screen no matter what tool you have selected. You can also rotate your images with the help of the **Transform** option. First select *Command + F* to enter the transform mode. Then move your cursor to just outside of the corner of the image to see the cursor icon change to a curved arrow. Now just drag the mouse to rotate the image to any angle. Also if you hold down the **Shift** key while rotating, it will rotate in five degree increments.

Sometimes you will need to flip a photo around to make the composition work better. It might be a landscape, a floral shot, or a background in a multiphoto collage. Whatever the reason, sometimes your image will look better when flipped on a vertical or horizontal axis. These options are also under the **Tool Options** menu of the Move Tool and in the main **Edit** menu.

Additional Move tool options

There are two final settings in the **Tool Options** menu of the Move Tool. You might want to leave them as checked, but just like many workflow items try it both ways and see what you like best:

- **Auto Select Layer**: The first option is called **Auto Select Layer**. This can help your workflow go much faster, but also sometimes it does take a little to get used to it. When you have multiple layers in the image and have this option checked, anytime you click on a layer it will make that layer the current active layer. It saves time from clicking on the layer in the **Layers** toolbar and helps make moving around different layers really quick. Sometimes though, you will have layers very close to each other, and having this on can cause you to accidentally activate the wrong layer, so it can be toggled on and off at any time.

- **Show Transform Controls**: The last setting is called Show Handles. This will automatically turn on the handles to transform a layer anytime you have that layer active and are in the Move tool. With this turned on, you don't need to go to the Transform tool to change the size of a layer. Just make the layer active, click the *V* key to select the Move Tool, and then start to drag the handles to adjust the size of your image.

The Marquee tools

The Marquee tools are the simplest of the different selection tools. There are four different types of Marquee tools, namely the **Rectangular Marquee**, **Elliptical Marquee**, **Column Marquee**, and **Row Marquee** tools. By default, only the Rectangular and Elliptical Marquees are shown in the toolbar, but you can add the other two anytime by going to the **Tool preferences** panel we talked about in the first chapter. These are great for selecting objects that are rectangular or oval shaped. Once you choose the Marquee tool, just drag an area over the image to make your selection. Also note, when using the **Elliptical Marquee** tool you can slightly smooth out edges by selecting the **Smooth Edges** option in the Elliptical Marquee tool settings menu. Once you make a selection you can easily modify your selection in the tool settings menu. You have four options for modifying the selections, as shown in the following screenshot. With these you can **Add To**, **Subtract**, or **Intersect** your selections to fine-tune them. By using these, you can refine and modify your selection until you get the exact selection you need, as shown in the following screenshot:

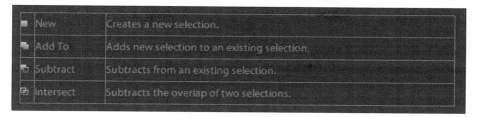

■	New	Creates a new selection.
⬛	Add To	Adds new selection to an existing selection.
⬜	Subtract	Subtracts from an existing selection.
⬛	Intersect	Subtracts the overlap of two selections.

Once you have made your selection you can refine the hardness of the edge or even transform the selection by going into the Tool settings menu. Here you will see a **Refine Selection** and **Transform Selection** option. Clicking on the **Refine Selection** button will let you change how smooth the selection is, the feather, and the size of the selection. It's useful when you have a selection that doesn't have a hard edge and you need to have a selection that is soft around the edges. In this example, we will copy the child's head and feather the selection to smooth it out. If you copy and paste this into another photo, it still won't be perfect since some of the background is still seen, but that can be easily erased later.

Here you can see the options that are available to refine a selection. Notice how the selection is soft around the child's head due to the **Feather** option:

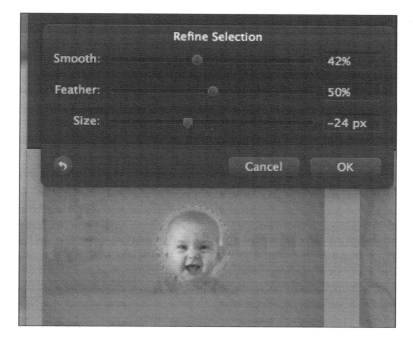

Before we get into the other ways of selecting an object, we should take a minute to review some helpful keyboard shortcuts:

- *Command + A*: This shortcut will select the entire canvas.
- *Command + D*: This is used to deselect your selection.
- *Command + Z*: Here you can go backwards if you made a mistake and need to return to a previous step. Keep clicking this button to go back as many steps as needed.
- *Shift + Command + Z*: This will let you redo any actions that you undid.
- *Command + C*: Once you make a selection, this will allow you to copy the selection to the clipboard.
- *Command + V*: After you copy something, this will let you paste the selection and will have it as a new layer.

You can also invert your selection by going to **Edit | Invert Selection**.

 If you need to select just the area of a specific layer, it is preferable to use the Load Selection shortcut. To do this, just hold down the *Command* key and click in the thumbnail of the layer. This automatically selects the contents of the layer.

The Lasso tools

When selecting objects in real life, you normally aren't going to have the luxury of having a rectangular or circular selection to make. For selecting objects that don't have a shape that would fit into the marquee tools, the lasso tool might be the best choice. There are two lasso tools, namely the Lasso tool and the Polygonal Lasso tool.

- **The Lasso tool**: Let's start with the Lasso tool and walk through how to best use this selection tool. First you can go to the Lasso tool with the keyboard shortcut *L*. The Lasso tool is the most helpful selection tool when making a free-form selection. Just click-and-drag your mouse around the image to make any type of free-form selection. If you get a little off the line that you are trying to select, don't worry; keep finishing the selection and then use the Add to or Subtract from tools we talked about previously to refine your selection.

- **The Polygonal Lasso tool**: This tool doesn't give you the total flexibility that the normal Lasso tool gives you, but it will still allow you to select items that have straight lines. Let's take this image of a building as an example. With the Polygonal Lasso tool, it's really quick and easy to select the building if we wanted to change out the sky. Just start at one point and click to set the starting point of your selection. Then start to move around the edge of the item; the tool draws a straight line, so every time you need to alter the direction of the selection, just click to set another point and continue along the edge. Once you are done you can go back to the starting point and click to finish the selection or double-click your mouse to finish.

In the following screenshot, you can see that by using the Polygonal Lasso tool you can make a selection on an image with many straight lines. This is a very quick way to make a selection when you mainly have straight lines on an image:

The Magic Wand tool

The Magic Wand tool is great when you have a selection area that has the same color. This can be great for removing the sky from an image or anytime where you have a solid color that you need to select. Let's take this image of a jellyfish and drop out the background so that we can change it out with something else. You can click on the Magic Wand Tool in the toolbar or enter the keyboard shortcut *W*. Before you get started, if your item has smooth edges, select **Smooth Edges** from the tool settings menu before making your selection. To make your selection just click on the background, and while holding down the mouse drag the mouse to change the tolerance of the selection. This will make the selection smaller or larger by changing how much tolerance you have from the initial point you clicked on.

In the following screenshot, the blue color in the background was clicked on to select most of the background. You can increase **Tolerance** here to include more of the blue color:

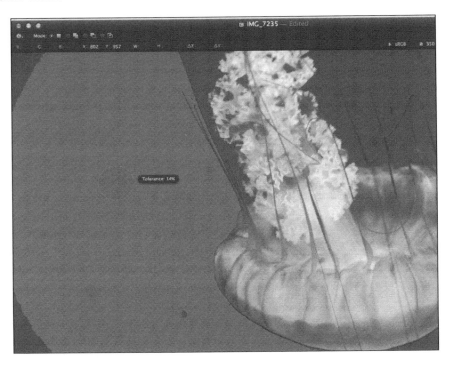

Make selection based on color

If you have the need to select part of an image that is all in one uniform color, this can be done with a quick click. This is very helpful if you photograph something against a very plain wall that has the same color and you need to remove that background. First click on **Edit | Select Color**. Your cursor will change to a magnifying glass and you can select any color. Here you can see that I am selecting the skin tone of the child's face as follows:

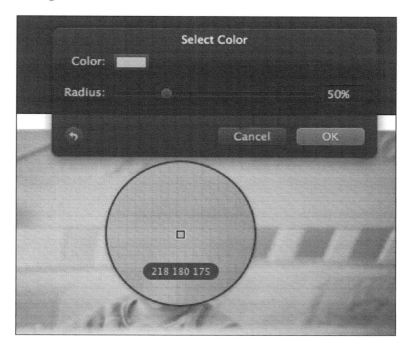

After you have selected the color, use the **Radius** slider to change **Tolerance** of the selection. As you slide this left and right, you will see the image change to black and white to give you a preview of what part of the image will be selected. The white parts will be included in the selection and the black parts will not, as shown in the following screenshot:

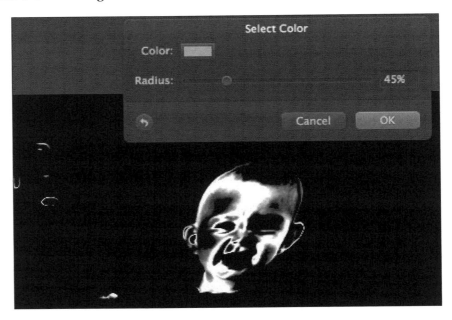

Use the Quick Mask mode

Often, with the use of the Magic Wand tool you still might have to refine certain edges. Say you have a person with frizzy hair and are using the Magic Wand to select the background. There might be some minor details in between the hair strands that you will want to manually refine. This is where quick masks come in and following is a quick step-by-step guide to use the Quick Mask mode.

- After you make the initial Magic Wand selection, go to the **Tools** submenu and click on the **Edit in Quick Mask Mode** button. This will turn on a mask that shows the unselected parts in red. You can also get to this mode by clicking on the keyboard shortcut *Q*.

- Now switch over to **Brush** and use a fine point brush set to white and paint on the red sections that you want to include in the selection. If you make a mistake, don't worry. You can change the color of the brush from white to black and paint back over to bring back the red overlay.

You can always set the default colors to the default, that is White and Black (as primary and secondary), by clicking the *D* key. Also you can switch between primary and secondary anytime by clicking on the *X* key.

- When you are in the Quick Mask mode, you can zoom in very close on your image to make very detailed selections. Once you are done, just click on the **Edit in Quick Mode** button in **Edit** again to go back to the normal selection view. Also you can edit using the Quick Mask mode in any selection tool and not just in the Magic Wand tool.

Summary

Selections are great because they allow you to choose only a certain part of an image to edit, leaving the rest of the image untouched. While it's easy to select a part of a photo and make a correction, such as changing the color or brightness, it's always a good practice to copy and paste that selection into its own layer before making changes. This way, if you mess up something you are only making adjustments on a new layer and can very easily delete that layer to start over. Having layers with specific selections will allow you to fine-tune your images in the most artistic way. Not every part of your image should have the same hue/saturation or many other attributes, so being able to select what you need to modify is the first part of creating that perfect image.

In this chapter, we learned all about the many ways of selecting parts of an image. In the next chapter we are going to dive into **Layers** so that we can start to create image composites.

3
All about Layers

Layers are one of the most powerful tools we have for editing our images. For those of you who haven't used an editing software with layers, such as Photoshop, it may be a completely new term, so let's take a quick minute to review what a layer is. The best way to think about a layer is like a stack of paper. You can stack pictures on top of pictures to create multi-image collages or to create textures or backgrounds for your images, and the sheets of paper can be opaque or even have cutouts to see completely through them. With a layer you can change the blending, which will affect how you see the layers that are beneath it. Layers make Pixelmator very powerful, and since you can create an unlimited amount of layers, there is really no limit to what you can create. By default, when you open up an image there will be just one layer titled *Layer*. You can always use the keyboard shortcut to show/hide the **Layers** menu by using the shortcut *command + 2*. In this chapter we will walk through all the options we have in the **Layers** menu, and see some real-world examples on how to get the most out of using layers.

Rearranging layers

Let's start with some simple navigation around the Layers panel. First, when looking at the **Layers** panel, the layers you have at the top of the panel will be shown above the other layers. So if you have a full-size photo of the canvas that has a normal blending mode, you won't be able to see anything beneath that layer. As you start to add layers to an image many times, you will need to rearrange the layers. Any layer can easily be moved by clicking and holding down on the layer and then dragging it to any other position.

Here you can see what the **Layers** panel looks like with a few layers for a multi-image collage:

You also will need to hide layers sometimes to quickly see what is beneath that layer. There is a checkbox on the right-hand side of the layer that you can check on or off to show or hide the layer. This is very useful to see the true impact that a layer has on the overall composition of the image.

If you need to fully delete a layer, click on the layer and then click on the - button at the very bottom-left of the **Layers** menu. You can also use the *Delete* key on your keyboard to delete the layer. Adding the new layers is just as simple; if you click the + button, it will create a new blank layer. Also, every time you copy and paste a photo in Pixelmator, it will automatically add that image as a new layer.

Using layer masks

Layers by themselves can be pretty powerful, but you can see the real power of this feature when creating layer masks. A layer mask is a way to hide certain parts of the layer without having to delete the entire layer. With a layer mask, you are creating an editable mask that uses black, white, and shades of grey to determine what is going to be visible in the image. If you use a layer mask and paint with black, it will make the area 100 percent transparent. Any part of the layer mask that is white will have no transparency, and layer masks that are grey will show the image at a transparency depending on the darkness/lightness of the shade of grey. Basically, any part of the image that you don't want to have visible can be painted with black on the layer mask, and parts to be shown fully can be left in white. Anything in between can be a shade of grey.

You can add a layer mask by right-clicking on the layer and choosing **Add Mask**. This will add a thumbnail of the mask to the right-hand side of the layer thumbnail in the **Layers** panel. It will be filled with white by default, and you can use any method you like to paint the areas you want to mask with black. We will now see a quick example of how you can use a layer mask to blend something, and at the end of the chapter we will walk through creating a real photo composite so you can see a common use of layer masks.

You will notice that the main layer is a solid blue color, but with the layer mask we have added a black-to-white gradient along the left side of the image. This makes the left side fully transparent and then it fades in such a way that it does not have any transparency where the layer mask is fully white.

Another thing you can do with a layer mask is apply filters to it. After you have created a layer mask and have it selected, go to the **Effects Browser** panel and select any effect. In the following example, let's create a layer mask over the sky and have a deep blue color layer below that. You can choose any photo you have that has the sky in it, and follow the steps along with this example:

1. First select the layer mask and then the Gradient tool.

2. Then apply the black-to-white gradient along the top of the image.

3. Now you can add an effect. In this example, select the layer mask and go to the **Effects Browser** panel.

4. Here I picked the **Hatched** effect in the **Halftone** section, which gives a bit of a pattern to the layer mask.

Grouping and merging layers

When you start creating a complicated composite image with lot of layers, you will want to group and merge your layers together to help keep things easily manageable. Sometimes you may end up with a huge list of layers and depending on the size of your monitor, you might not be able to see all of the layers without scrolling in the panel. That can be a pain, and also make it hard to find the exact layer that you want to start editing. With Pixelmator, you can create a group of layers that is basically a folder in your **Layers** panel containing multiple layers inside.

With a group, you can expand/collapse the folder according to the need to see or hide the layers inside it. Let's do a quick walkthrough on how to group layers together. In the following example, there is an image with many layers. To make things easy to manage, let's group together different layers to organize them. In this specific example, it's an album layout and the file has items that are used as background graphics. These would make a good layer group, so I will start by selecting these layers. To select multiple layers, you can click *Shift* on the layers that are next to each other and then click *command* on the last two layers at the bottom. Once you have selected the images that you want to group, click on the Actions drop-down menu at the bottom of the **Layers** panel and select the **Group Layers** option. Here is what that menu will look like:

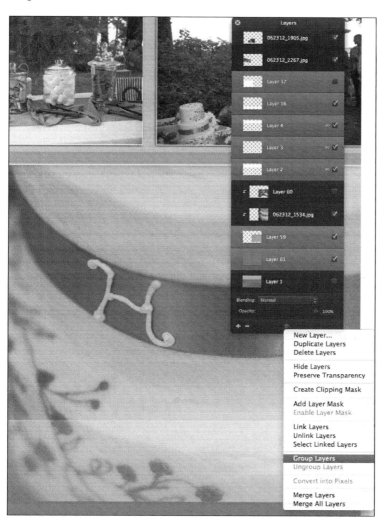

This will move all selected layers into one group. You can easily expand the group by clicking on the small arrow at the left of the group you want to expand. You will also want to name the group so you can identify what's inside. Double-click on the name to edit the name. In this example, we will name it `Background Images`:

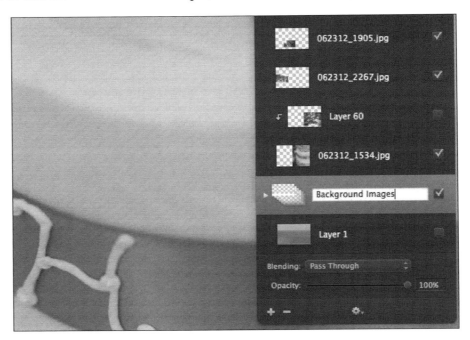

With layers, you also will want to move their order around so that items are grouped in a way that makes sense to you. Moving around layers is easy; you can click-and-drag any layer to any position in the **Layers** panel. Also, when you are creating an image composite with multiple images many times, you will spend a lot of time getting the position of layers just right. It might be a sequence of images that are all lined up in just the right way and you want to make sure that those layers remain in that specific sequence. Pixelmator has the ability to link layers together so that whenever you move one layer in the set of linked layers, they will all move together. This is another option that will be available after you select multiple layers in the Actions drop-down menu that is at the bottom of the **Layers** panel. Just select the layers you would like to link, and in the Actions drop-down menu select the **Link Layers** option. Once you link the layers together, you will notice a very small link icon that can be seen on the layers to the right-hand side of the layer name.

Blending modes to merge layers together

The different blending modes that layers have are key to effectively merging together images. With each layer, you can set a **Blending** mode that will determine how a layer blends with the pixels on the layers that are underneath. Sometimes you can use this to make a layer lighter or darker or to change the color of a layer.

There are almost 30 different blending modes. The blending modes can be accessed for each layer by going to the very bottom of the **Layers** panel and clicking on the **Blending** drop-down menu. The blending modes are separated into six categories by simple line breaks in the drop-down menu.

The main types of blending modes are:

- **Basic**
- **Darken**
- **Lighten**
- **Contrast**
- **Comparative and Hue**
- **Saturation and Lightness**

The **Darken** option makes the interacting pixels darker and the **Lighten** options makes them lighter. The **Contrast** blending option can be used to increase or decrease the contrast between interacting pixels. The options in the **Comparative and Hue** section will invert the color of interacting pixels and give some pretty crazy effects. Finally, the **Comparative and Hue**, **Saturation and Lightness** modes apply specific color changes.

In the following example, you will see a file with two layers: the top layer is a photo of a flower and at the bottom is a beach scene. The layers are set to 100 percent opacity, so when the **Blending** mode is set to **Normal** you can't see the layer beneath:

Now compare that to the following image. Here, the **Blending** mode was changed to **Darken**. Now only certain parts of the background image are showing through:

Finally compare the previous two photos to the following one. Here, the **Blending** mode was changed to **Lighten**. You can see how blending modes will let you drastically change the way your layers interact with each other.

The best way to really get a good hand on all of these different modes is to play around and try it out. Create a file with two layers and try out each blending mode to experiment and see how this changes your image.

Using layers to create a photo-composite image

Let's put everything we just learned to real-world use and create a simple photo composite. I want to take the following two images and blend them together so we can take the wonderful clouds from the first photo and merge them into the waterway photo, which has a very plain blue sky. Here are our two starting images:

First, I will use the rectangular marquee tool to select a portion of the sky from the image with the clouds and then copy this selection by using the shortcut *command + C*. Then I'll change over to the waterway photo and paste the cloud selection in this photo by using the shortcut *command + V*. Whenever you paste an image in another, it will automatically create a new layer; so now I have the original background layer of the waterway photo plus a new layer with the clouds. Since the sizing of the two images are different, the photo of the clouds doesn't fit the entire frame. So I'll use the **Transform Selection** tool to make the width of the cloud layer match the background layer, as follows:

Next, we will want to blend these images together, and the easiest way to do this is to add a layer mask on the cloud layer. Once you create a layer mask, select the Gradient tool and choose a white-to-black gradient. Start dragging from the top of the image downwards and you will see how the gradient starts to affect the image. Drag down until slightly above the horizon.

Viola! A really quick and easy way to blend two images together.

Summary

In this chapter we learned what layers are and the ways in which you can organize layers for an effective workflow. We also went over what the different blending options are, and how you can use layer masks and blending modes to create multi-image compositions. With a good understanding of working with layers, you are now on your way to unleash the creative artist inside. In the next chapter we will cover the **Effects Browser** panel, which is used to artistically edit our photos.

4

Using the Effects Browser Tools

In this chapter we will cover an overview of all Pixelmator's main sections of effects. Here we will learn how to use effects to artistically edit photos.

Pixelmator has many built-in effects that you can use to stylize your images and create artistic effects. In this chapter we are going to walk through all of the main effect sections and give you some insight about what you can do to artistically edit your images. First, if the **Effects Browser** panel isn't open, you can click **View** | **Show Effects** or press *Command + 3* to open it up. This tool panel has a drop-down at the very top of the toolbar that allows you to sort by the different sections of effects they have. In the center of the toolbar, you will see the available effects. A nice touch that Pixelmator has is that you can move your mouse over the thumbnails of available effects to see what that effect does. Move your mouse side to side on the preview to see what effect the filter has. To use an effect just double-click on the thumbnail to open up additional settings for that **Filter** and apply it. There are many effects that Pixelmator has that help you artistically edit your photos, and we will walk through all of the effect options in this chapter.

When using filters, remember that they are destructive, meaning that the changes you make to the image can't simply be brushed away, like when painting on or off a layer mask. It's always best to first duplicate the layer so you are working on a copy of the layer and then make any adjustments. Then if you make a mistake, just delete the layer to start over.

Using blur effects

The blur effects do just what the name suggests; it gives you a few different ways to add a blur effect to your images. There are six different blur filters, and we will go through what each one of these does.

Gaussian blur

One of the most popular types of blur, the Gaussian blur, is a very effective way of creating a natural looking blur in your image. This type of blur gives your image an overall soft feel. This is always a great way to apply a blur to a selected part of your image to give it a feeling of depth. When you use the **Gaussian** tool you will be able to set the radius of the image; this will control how much of a blur the effect causes. This will apply to the entire layer that you are on, but by using layer masks, you can have the blur effect only certain parts of your image. For example, let's say that you have a photo with a very small aperture and most of the image is in focus. You can easily create some depth by following these simple steps:

1. First duplicate the layer so you have two layers of the image.

2. Next, apply a **Gaussian** filter and adjust the **Radius** option to specify how much of a blur you would like.

3. Now apply a layer mask and use the graduated filter to have the blur only apply to a part of the image. In the following example, the blur is only applied to the bottom part of the image to give the photo a bit more dimension:

Motion blur

The **Motion** effect gives you a blur that simulates the feeling of motion. With this effect, you can not only select the **Radius** option to control how much blur happens, but you can also set angle of the blur. With this blur type, you can simulate the blur that you get when moving the camera while taking a long exposure photo.

Zoom blur

The **Zoom** effect is similar to the **Motion** effect in that it will simulate motion: but instead of giving the feel of the camera panning a scene, this effect simulates zooming the lens while taking a long exposure photo. When you select this tool, you will be able to set the **Radius** option to control the amount of blur but will also see a circle that you can move around the image. This will control where the center point of the zoom is going to be. In the following example, you can see how you can control the center point of the **Zoom** tool:

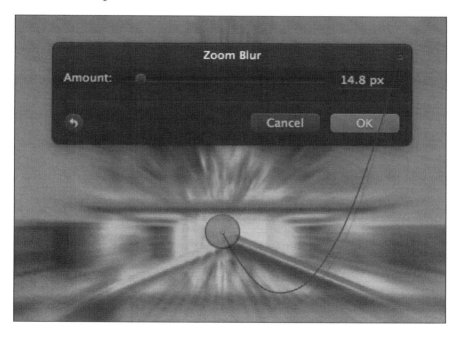

Median blur

The **Median** effect doesn't have any settings and is designed to help reduce noise in your image. What it will do is figure out the median value for a group of neighboring pixels and replace each pixel's value with the median.

Soften blur

The **Soften** effect can also be used to reduce noise. This effect has a setting to control the color noise level so you can reduce the color noise in an image. Here you can adjust the softness of the color noise on a slider from 0 to 100 percent. Setting it at 100 percent will be the maximum amount of softness to the color noise. You can control the sharpness of the image also with a slider from 0 to 100 percent.

Miniaturize blur

The **Miniaturize** effect is a cool way to create a tilt-shift type of look for a photo. When you open up this effect you will see two options, **Linear** and **Elliptical** (types of blur). With **Linear**, you will have a blur on the top and bottom of the image that fades into the middle. In the **Miniaturize** blur settings, you will see a circle in the center that you can move to adjust the center part of the image that will be in focus. You can also use the black circle on the left to adjust how far you want the blur to extend to in the image.

In the following example, the linear miniaturize blur effect is selected to create a blur along the top and bottom edges of the photo:

You also have control over the amount of the **Blur** by using the slider to go from 0 to 100 percent and setting the transition. The **Transition** option will let you control how hard or soft the blur transition is. If you set it on the low end of the scale, there will be a sharp change in the blur. The image will go from blurry to sharp in a very short transition; whereas if you set it to a higher level, there will be a more gradual transition from blurry to sharp.

Working with distortion effects

There are 15 different types of distortion effects. These will give you some carnival-style effects where you can make people's heads look really large or tiny. The distortion effects can give you some fun ways to play around with your images, but for professional use, these filters don't have as much value as some of the other effects you can use. Here is a rundown of the 15 different filters you can use in the distort section of the effects browser.

Bump

The **Bump** effect creates a bump at a certain point in the image. With this effect, you can pinpoint where the bump should appear as well as the size and scale of the bump. You can use this on a portrait of someone to create some very funny-looking effects by putting the bump on different parts of their face to create different distortions. It's a great way to edit a photo of someone for a funny gift.

Linear bump

The bump created by this effect isn't a circular bump but instead a bump line that goes through the entire image.

Pinch

The **Pinch** effect creates an area that pinches pixels inward. When you click on this effect, you can set the center point where the image will be pinched toward the circle and modify the **Radius** and **Scale** options. The larger the radius the more the image will zoom out, and the smaller the radius the closer you will zoom to the center. The **Scale** effect will set how much the image will be pinched. This is set on a scale of 0 to 100 percent. This is another one of those funny carnival type filters that can give you some pretty crazy results.

In the following screenshot, you can see how selecting the point of the pinch effect to be a the center of the child's face pinches the entire face towards the nose:

Hole

The **Hole** effect creates an actual hole in the image. It doesn't fill the hole with anything, so if this is your only layer, you will have a blank hole. Then it moves the pixels that were in the hole outward, distorting the pixels closest to the circle.

Ripple

This effect is a transition effect that only works with two layers. It creates a circular wave that moves outwards from the center point, revealing the new image in the wake of the wave.

Page curl

This gives you the look of a page curling and gives you a 3D look. You can set the **Angle** and **Radius** options, and with this effect, give any corner of the page a curling effect.

Capsule

The **Capsule** effect is a cool effect that might not have much real-world use if you are editing a photo, but it is an easy and fun tool to use to create a round-edged button. It wraps the image around a pill-shaped capsule. If you create a simple document with a color gradient, apply this filter to create a simple 3D-looking button.

Creating a button is simple; here, you can see a sample button and how to control the radius and refraction of the button using the **Radius** and **Refraction** options:

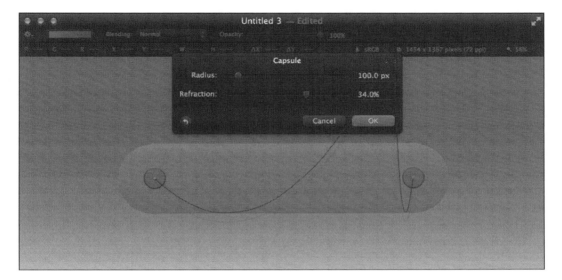

Glass ring

This effect creates a ring that simulates glass by distorting the section in the glass ring.

Circle splash

This will allow you to set the diameter of a circle that will remain sharp. Everything outside the circle will have a motion effect that makes it look like the lens is being zoomed.

Displacement

The **Displacement** effect applies the grayscale values of a second image to the first image.

Glass

This will give you a glass-like texture to your image. To add texture to a background image or just to give a part of the image a texture, this effect works well.

Bar swipe

This is another transition effect and will transit from one image to another by passing a bar over the source image.

Twirl

The **Twirl** effect will rotate pixels around a point to produce a swirling effect, with the size of the twirl and angle customizable.

Vortex

This effect is similar to ('but not as drastic as) the **Twirl** effect, and will rotate the pixels around a point to simulate a vortex.

Circular wrap

This effect turns your image into a circle and adds a motion blur to the circle. It's like taking your photo and spinning it on a wheel to make it appear like a circle.

Using sharpen effects

Sharpening your image is always an important part of the post-processing process, and especially before sending something off to be printed. Depending on your settings with your **Digital single-lens reflex (DSLR)** camera, your camera might be doing some sharpening in the processing it does in-camera, or it might be doing very little. Depending on what your subject is, you might want to have the final print as tack sharp as it can be, and applying some sharpening to the photo before it's printed is probably a good idea. There are three types of sharpening effects you can apply to your images:

- **Sharpen**
- **Edges**
- **Unsharp**

The **Sharpen** option will simply increase the image detail by sharpening the entire image. You will be able to set this sharpening amount on a scale of 0-100.

The **Edges** option will find all of the edges in an image and automatically sharpen them. You can't adjust the amount here at all; it simply makes all of your edges sharper.

The **Unsharp** option will give your image a sharper look by increasing the contrast of the edges between different-colored pixels in an image.

Learning the color adjustment effects

In the **Color Adjustments** section you will be able to carry out all of your color balance changes and conversions to black and white. There are three main sections here; we will start with the first, which covers the basic photo adjustments. At the top of the **Color Adjustments** section, you will see six filters to control the basics of your image. The first option you have here is **Auto Enhance**, will use an algorithm to make what edits the program thinks your image needs to be perfect. Like many automated things, sometimes this works and improves your images, while sometimes it can make your image look much worse. I am always a big believer in staying away from anything automated in photography; it won't always get your image to be perfect, plus you really don't learn anything when using automated methods.

The next option that you have is to adjust the brightness of the image. Here you can adjust the brightness of the image (from dark to light and vice versa) as well as the contrast of the image.

Adjusting levels

Levels are a very powerful tool for your image editing. The **Levels** option allows you to change the values of shadows, mid-tones, and highlights in an image. When you open up the **Levels** effect, you will see a histogram with three pinpoints at the bottom of the image. The point on the very left will allow you to adjust the shadows of the image, and any of these values can be adjusted by simply dragging the point to the right or left of the histogram. The center point lets you adjust the mid-tones of the image, and the right hand point lets you effect the white point and highlights of the image.

A very good tip to easily adjust your image is to adjust the **Black** and **White** points to make the edges of the histogram hit the very bottom. This will improve the overall exposure and contrast of the image. See the following screenshot for an example:

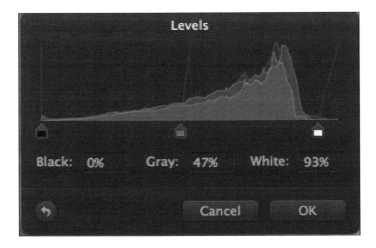

Adjusting curves

The **Curves** effect comes next, and this is a useful tool to adjust the entire tonal range of your image. You can also use the **Curves** effect to adjust the **Red, Green,** or **Blue** layers directly and create interesting color effects. Similar to the **Levels** effect, when you change the lower left of the curve, this will affect the dark values in your image. If you change the center, it will affect the mid-tones most, and changes on the right side will affect the lightest values in your image.

By default, the line will always be a 45-degree angle moving up from left to right. You can click on the curve to add a point and then drag that point up or down to adjust that tonal range up or down.

To remove a point, hit *Command* and click on the curve point. If you want to increase the contrast of an image, you would want to have an S-curve that looks similar to the following example. What this is basically doing is changing the darks to be darker and then making the whites whiter:

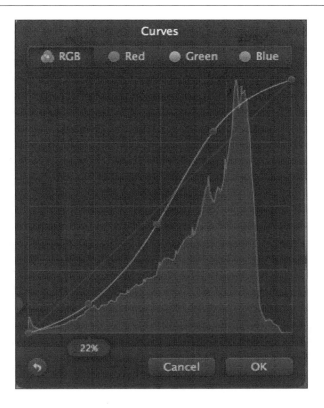

Adjusting exposure

The **Exposure** effect is a straightforward way to make the overall image darker or lighter. Move the slider to the left to make the image darker and to the right to lighten the image.

Using the Light and Dark effect

The **Light and Dark** effect will allow you to adjust just the shadows or highlights in an image. This is very helpful since all digital cameras are limited in the range of tones that they can capture. Often, in a situation with a lot of contrast, you will capture the highlights well but the shadows will go too dark, or vice versa. With this effect, you have two sliders, one to lighten the shadows and the other to darken the highlights. The great thing about each one of these is that when you lighten the shadows, for example, this will only lighten the shadow areas of the image and won't lighten any other part of the image so you can selectively update only a certain tone in the image.

Adjusting color tones

In the next section with six filters you can modify more specific color effects. The first filter here is called **Hue** and will let you effect the hue and saturation of the image. An advantage of this is that you can adjust the overall hue and saturation of the entire image or choose a specific color to adjust in the **Colors** tab. Selecting this effect will open up a new panel with six colors at the top. Clicking on any of these colors will allow you to apply that specific color only. You can also tighten the color range of what you are adjusting by moving the handles on the color wheel closer. In this example, we will adjust just the yellow color of the flower. First click on the orange-yellow color at the very top of the window; this will limit the colors we are adjusting to the range shown on the left part of the following image. Here you can see it will adjust more than just yellow since this range also includes some green and orange, which we don't want. If I leave it like this and adjust the hue it will adjust the yellow flower but also some of the green leaves behind it. If you click-and-drag the handles on the circle and make the color range tighter, you can adjust it to look like the right part of the image where it's now limited to just a yellow range:

To adjust hue for the entire image, just drag the dots around the color wheel to select the colors to modify.

Colorize

The next effect, **Colorize**, and will let you tone the image by using a color wheel similar to the **Hue** filter. Just drag the dot around the color wheel to tone the image, and then use the saturation and lightness sliders to set how saturated you want the tone to be.

Replace color

The **Replace Color** effect does just what its name implies. It gives you a way to replace the color of your image with something else. Start by clicking on the **Color** box at the very top of this effect and then point your mouse to the color in the image you would like to replace. Click on this color and it will enter the color box. You can then set the **Radius** option, which will control the extent of the radius around the color you clicked on that will be affected If the range is very low, only that specific color will be adjusted, while if you set a higher range, close variations of that color will also be adjusted. As you move the **Radius** slider back and forth you will see the image changes into a mask so you can see exactly what is going to be effected. Here the parts of the image that appear to be white in the mask will be affected, while the black pixels are not going to be touched by any changes.

Color balance

The **Color Balance** effect gives you the ability to change the **Cyan/Red, Magenta/Green**, and **Yellow/Blue** colors. First you can select the tonal range of the image you want to edit, either the shadows, mid-tones, or highlights. Then, drag the sliders to adjust the colors as you need to.

Channel mixer

The **Channel Mixer** effect can also be used to tone your images. In the **Channel Mixer** palette, first select the **Output channel** that you want to blend into another color channel. Here you can pick the **Red, Green**, or **Blue** channel. Then, to decrease the color's contribution to the channel, you can drag the slider to the left. To increase it drag the slider to the right.

Invert

The final effect in this middle section of the **Color Adjustments** panel is **Invert**. There aren't any settings for this effect; it will just completely invert all of the colors of your image.

Black-and-white adjustments and toning

The last section in the **Color Adjustments** panel gives you three options. The first option is **Desaturate** and will take the saturation of the image down to zero. This gives you a simple way of creating a black-and-white image but usually will give you a fairly flat image. If you want to create a nice-looking black-and-white image, you'd have much more control and can get a richer black-and-white result by using the next effect, the **Black and White** effect. Here you will see a color wheel at the top that you can turn around, adjusting the way that certain colors are changed when converted. Beneath that, you can change the brightness and contrast and even add some grain to the image to go for a real black and white film look.

The final effect in this section is the sepia tone where you can give your photo an old-fashioned sepia look.

Overview of Tile effects

The **Tile** effects section gives you 15 different effects that tile the image to create a pattern. The effects available here are **Kaleidoscope**, **Triangle**, **Brickwork**, **Hexagon**, **Pinwheel**, **Bug Eye**, **Shutters**, **Windmill**, **Snowflake**, **Funhouse**, **Tessera**, **Perspective**, **Affine Clamp**, **Affine**, and **Mirror**.

These are useful to help with creating backgrounds. If you start off with a solid color layer or a gradient color, go through each one to see exactly how they affect your image and the interesting patterns that you can create with these.

Using Stylize effects

The **Stylize** section of effects gives you many different ways to stylize your image with effects such as **Crystalize…**, **Pixelate...**, **Snow…**, **Vintage…**, and many others. Here is an overview of the different filters you have in the stylize section and what they do:

- **Crystallize**: This effect will create polygon-shaped color blocks
- **Honeycomb**: This displays an image as colored hexagons
- **Pixelate**: This will create a pixelated effect for the image that you can increase the intensity of to make it look like a retro, 8-bit type of image
- **Noise**: This adds noise to an image

- **Rain**: This simulates rain drops
- **Snow**: This effect simulates snowflakes
- **Vintage**: This effect creates an aged image effect
- **Twilight**: This effect will darken the image, and based on the intensity you select, can create a very soft and dark image
- **Fog**: This effect will soften the image and give an overall glow
- **Gloom**: This will soften only the highlight areas of your photo
- **Spotlight**: With the spotlight effect, you can apply a spotlight to the image
- **Coating**: This effect produces a shaded image from a mask
- **Edge Work**: This creates a black and white relief image
- **Sketch**: The sketch effect will create an outline of your image that looks like a sketch with a black pen
- **Edges**: Edges will find all of the edges in your image and display them in color
- **Comic**: This creates a comic book style effect for your image by outlining the edges and applying a halftone color effect
- **Threshold**: This effect will change colors to extreme high-contrast, giving you a black and white high contrast effect

The Halftone effects

Halftone refers to a reprographic technique that will give you the appearance of a continuous tone by using all dots. The dots can vary in size, shape, or spacing, but the entire image is made up of dots. With the **Halftone** effects in Pixelmator, you have five different types of **Halftone** effects you can apply, namely, **Circular**, **Hatched**, **Line**, **Dot**, and **CMYK**. You can use these to create texture over your images or to create backgrounds.

The Generator effects

The effects under the **Generator** section give you nine different effects to generate items in your images, such as **Sunbeams**, **Starbursts**, **Clouds**, and even a **Random** effect if you want to roll the dice and see what random effect you can apply to the image.

Additional effects under the other menu

In the final section of effects, the **Other** section, you have 54 more effects that you can use. We are not going to walk through each one of these and what they do here, but many of the effects will give you options for artistic things that you can do to the image, such as giving it an old photo sepia look or a solarize look. You might not use these in day-to-day use with your images, but there probably is just the right effect for a random project that you might be working on some day. Spend a little time going through all of these and have some fun playing around! With filters, there are many creative ways that you can edit your photos; don't forget to experiment and have fun!

In this chapter we covered many of the creative filters that you can apply to your image in Pixelmator. There are very many filters; you can let your creative mind run wild and have fun. Here you see a small example of some of the filters we covered in the chapter; take some time to review each filter one by one and see just how they can effect many different types of photos. In the next chapter, we will cover some additional tools Pixelmator has to creatively edit photos.

5

More Creative Photo
Corrections

In this chapter we are going to get into some more advanced tools that you can use to get creative with your photos. We will cover lots of cool features such as the clone stamp tool and using text and gradients to enhance your digital artwork.

Using the clone stamp tool

The clone stamp tool is essential for retouching and removing unwanted items from your photos. It's a great way to copy part of an image to another part and it does have many uses. Once you get the hang of this tool, it might be one of your favorites for retouching. First, you can get started by clicking on the S key on your keyboard or selecting the stamp tool in the main tool menu.

Let's use the following beach photo as an example. If we want to remove some of the leaves in the sand, we can paint them away with the clone stamp tool. For this example, let's remove the leaf that is in the center of the image. The first time you click on the tool with an image, it will turn your cursor into a circle and prompt you with the **Click on an area to define the source clone** message. I'll click on an area of the sand to the right-hand side of the leaf that is of the same texture that you want to replace. This will be my source that will be used to paint over the leaf. The key to getting it to work well is to select the correct type of brush. Generally, for removing items you will want a fairly large and soft brush. To select a new brush, just click on the Brushes icon at the top-left corner of the screen and select a soft brush from the brush list.

For more information on brushes and creating your own custom brush presets, see the very end of this chapter.

Once you select a brush, start clicking to paint over the leaf and clone the area that you first selected. As you move the cursor, the area you had selected as the source will move with you, so pay careful attention to the area that is being cloned. When you get to a point where you are cloning something you don't want to, then you can always set a new starting area for the source clone. To do this, just click on the target-like icon that is at the top-left corner of the main screen right next to the gear icon. Then select any part of the image to set a new source clone.

The following is the edited image with the leaf in the middle cloned out:

Another very quick way of removing unwanted images is using the **healing tool**. This automates the entire process of removing an unwanted item from the scene. In many scenes, if you are removing something that is set on a background that has a uniform design such as sand, grass, or a textured wall, it can work flawlessly and can be a very quick way of removing items. However, if the item you are removing is set against something that isn't a textured background, it might give you better results to use the stamp tool or something else.

To use the healing tool, click on the Band-Aid-like icon in the toolbar. Then click and paint over the image you would like to remove and watch it do its magic! Another way you can use the healing tool is by creating a selection by using any of the selection tools. Once you have the selection ready, click on the healing tool. If you click on the tool setting menu, the first option will be **Heal Selection**. Click on this to heal the selection you have. In the following screenshot, you can see how to simply select the middle leaf and heal the selection:

Using shapes

Shapes can come in very handy when you are creating a composition and need to add some design elements to your image. There are six different built-in shapes that come with Pixelmator; they are as follows:

- Rectangle
- Ellipse
- Rounded Rectangle
- Polygon
- Line
- Star

These can also be used as a great way to call out some text on an image by having it inside a shape. Let's take a look at how to create a shape. After you click on the toolbar, double-click on it to open up the options of available shapes and choose the shape you would like to use.

At the very top of the image window you will see a list of different options. Walking through these from the left-hand side you'll find different things you can customize:

- First, you will see a drop-down list that allows you to either draw a new shape or add to an existing shape.
- Next, you can have a color to fill the shape, check the box next to **Fill**, and then click on the color box to open up a color selector.
- Next, you can set a stroke to the shape. If you aren't familiar with this term, it's just an outline around the shape.
- After this, you can set the pixel size of the outline and also the color.
- The next option you have is to include a drop shadow in the shape.

Once you turn any of these options on, you can set additional settings under the **Shape Settings** button. This will pop up additional options for the stroke and shadow on the shape. The following screenshot is a view of the shape settings you can adjust:

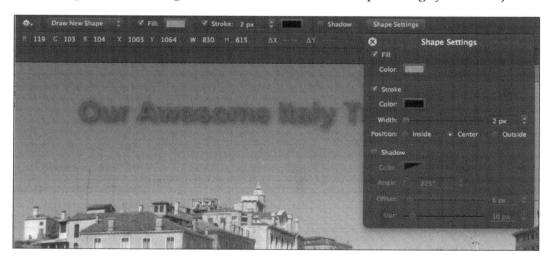

Once you create a shape, you will be able to edit the shape anytime by clicking on the layer and then using the bounding boxes on the corners of the shape to drag and resize the shape. Also, for the rounded rectangle tool, you will also see another small blue circle at the top-left side of the shape. If you click on this and drag it back and forth, this will allow you to adjust the size or the round edge of the rectangle.

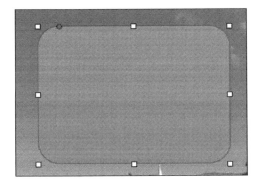

How to use text

Adding text with Pixelmator is quick, but at the same time gives you a good amount of control over the look of the font. Start by clicking on the *T* key or the text icon in the toolbar to open up the text tool.

You will see a toolbar of options show up at the top of the image window and a textbox that you can start typing into. Change any of the font properties, such as font type, font options, size, and other font options. Then start typing away to create your text. If at anytime you need to update the text, just click within the text area and it becomes editable. The following screenshot is what a textbox looks like once you have entered in some text:

Pixelmator doesn't have built-in text filters that other editing programs (such as Photoshop) have, but, that doesn't mean there aren't some easy ways to create cool custom text effects. First let's review one of the most common text effects, that is, creating a drop shadow. Creating a drop shadow can be done in a few quick steps that we will walk through here.

1. First, right-click on the layer or *Control* + click **Duplicate**.
2. Then change the name of this layer to shadow so it's easier to recognize later.
3. Move this layer underneath the main text layer.
4. Then right-click on the layer and select **Convert into Pixels**. This will allow you to apply any effects to the text layer, just like you can with a regular layer.
5. Once it's been converted, apply a Gaussian blur effect to the shadow layer. For this example I used a 10-px blur.
6. Finally, with the **Move tool** you can move the shadow text slightly to offset it.

It's an easy way to create a nice-looking drop shadow to your text and give it some depth, as shown in the following screenshot:

While we are talking about customizing text, let's also add an inner shadow to this text. I'll use the same text we used previously but will change the text color from white to blue first, so that we can see the effects of the inner shadow. The first step is to create a blank new layer and name it Inner Shadow. Next, select the text from the main text layer. To select this, *Command* + click on the thumbnail of the main text layer and it will automatically select the text.

Next, navigate to **Edit | Refine Selection** and change the size to **-1**. Now, while still in the new layer, we will create a stroke. Select black as the color, and then for this text I am using a 5-px width. The position on the stroke should be set to **Inside**, and **Opacity** around 40 percent:

Finally, apply a Gaussian blur to this to soften the stroke; the size of the blur will depend on the size of the text. Here I am using a 4.8-px Gaussian blur. Now we have a nice inner shadow to the text:

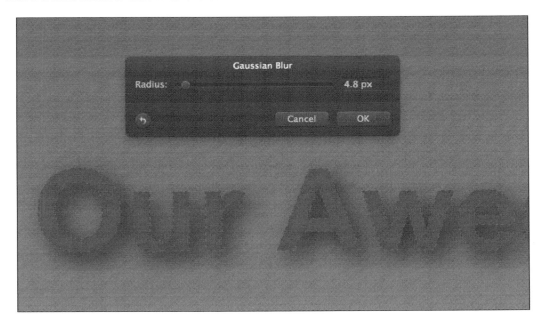

Using gradients and fill for backgrounds

Adding gradients and using the paint bucket tool to fill an area can be a good way to create backgrounds. For portrait photography, often you might need to create a collage of images to tell a more complete story of the portrait shoot for your client. This can be done the traditional way by printing separate images and then matting and framing the set of images into one frame, or this can be done digitally and then printed out on any type of medium, such as a canvas or a metal for a more unique look. The fill tool is a great way to fill white space with a color, and we will start with some basics on using this tool. First, select the paint bucket in the toolbar. To select your color, you can either click on the small color box at the top of the tool options bar or use the *Shift + Command + C* shortcut key to open up the color picker. The color picker gives you a few different ways to select a color, but a great way to get a custom color that matches the pallet of your image is to click on the magnifying glass icon on the top-left corner of the color toolbar. This turns your cursor into a larger magnifying glass and you can click on any part of the image to sample that color. In this example, you can see the magnifier on the pink crib background; once you click on any area, it will sample that color.

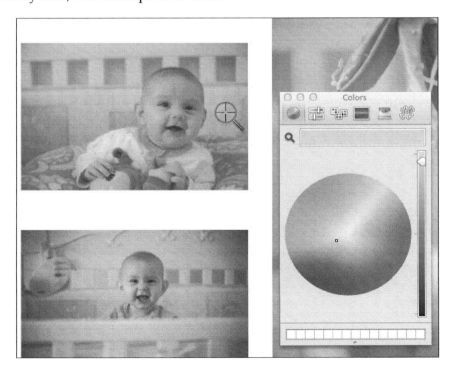

When you are ready to fill an area, select the **Blending** option at the top tool options bar and the **Opacity** option of the fill and click in the area to fill.

A simple fill might not be enough though, you might want to fill the area with a gradient color. The gradient tool is to the left-hand side of the fill tool in the toolbar, or can be accessed by the hotkey of *G*. When you bring up this tool, first click on the small color box at the top of the tool options bar or use the *Command + 5* shortcut key to open up the gradient toolbar. In this toolbar, you will be able to pick from a set of many predefined gradients or even set up your own custom gradients. Creating your own gradients can be fun and is really easy to do. So let's start with creating our own custom gradient:

1. First, click on the gear icon in the **Gradients** toolbar and select **New Gradient...**:

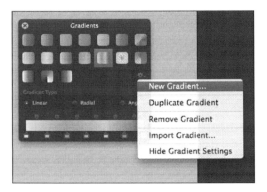

2. This starts you off with a simple black-to-white gradient. To change the color of the start or endpoint, just click on the small box at the bottom of the toolbar to open up a color picker and select your color. Once you have the start and endpoints selected, you can use the arrow at the top of the gradient bar and slide this back and forth to set where the fade happens:

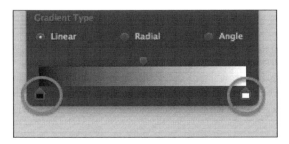

3. You can also create as many additional color points as you would like on the gradient by clicking inside the gradient bar where you would like the new color to be introduced. If you need to remove any of these points, just right-click on the gradient and select **Remove Color Stop**.

Now that you have your gradient colors set, click where you would like the gradient to start, and while holding down the mouse, drag to where you would like to see the gradient end. You will see it getting created in real time, which is very helpful to get the exact placement you would like. Once you have it all set, release the mouse and you are all done!

Using brushes

Brushes are used in many different areas of Pixelmator. You might use a brush to simply paint something onto a scene, or you might also use brushes in a layer mask to hide a certain area of an image. Here we will walk through the Brushes toolbar and give you a good feel of how to work with the settings for brushes.

First let's open up the brushes toolbar by navigating to **View | Show Brushes** or using the *Command + 4* shortcut key.

A good way to get a handle on brushes and the differences between the different types of brushes is to start with a blank canvas and select the brush tool choosing black as your color. Then paint onto the canvas with all of the different preset brushes to see the difference between all of these.

The default brush set includes some very basic brushes, but Pixelmator does have a few additional brush sets that they provide you with. To access these other brush presets, click on the gear icon from the brush toolbar and select from any of the brush sets they provide, including **Abstract**, **Artistic**, **Default**, **Grunge**, **Nature**, **Smoke**, and **Sparkle**. Play around with the defaults first to get a feel of what they look like and how you might be able to apply them to your artwork.

You can also create your own brush. To do this, click on the gear icon in the brush toolbar and choose the **Show Brush Settings** option at the bottom. This will open up many options that you can customize to create your own brush preset. Here you can change basic things about the brush, such as the diameter and the hardness, to more advanced things such as Jitter. The **Jitter** basically means randomness, so if you see the value of **Size**, **Stroke**, **Angle**, or **Opacity** in the Jitter section each time you use the brush, it will be slightly different. This helps if you are stamping a shape onto your image to fill a background but want a bit of randomness to show up in each brush. Take some time and play around with each one of these sliders to see how it affects the brush. You will always see a live preview of the brush at the very bottom.

The following screenshot is a view of the brush settings toolbar and all of the things you can control:

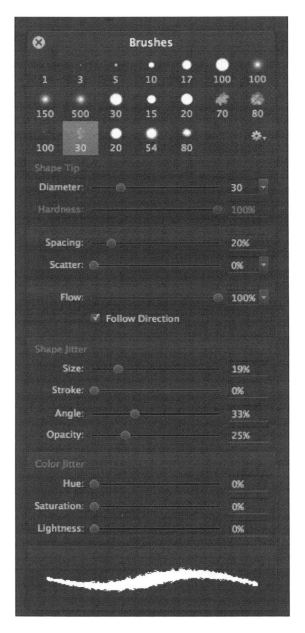

Another fun thing you can do with brushes is create a custom brush by copying another image. In the following example, let's use a photo of a leaf that was set against a white background. We can make a brush out of this so that it can be turned into a stamp, and add this into any image; it's really easy. To create a custom brush, perform the following steps:

1. Click on the gear icon in the brush toolbar and select **New Brush From Image**.

2. Select your image and it will appear in your brush's presets.

3. From here you can make the brush smaller or larger and control any of the other brush settings.

Any custom brushes that are created can also be used with the eraser tool.

Importing from Photoshop

If you have used Photoshop in the past and have a set of custom brushes for Photoshop, you can import those into Pixelmator. Click on the gear icon at the bottom of the brushes toolbar and then click on **Import Brushes**. Find the Photoshop presets and click on them in the **Import** dialog box. Just one step and now you can have all of your Photoshop brushes in Pixelmator!

Summary

In this chapter, we have learned how to use some of the advanced editing tools, such as the clone stamp and the healing brush. We also covered tools to use with design elements such as text, custom shapes, and background fill. With these tools, you will be able to start customizing your images and adding additional design elements to your work. In the next chapter, we will cover some real-world tutorials to put everything together and learn some more advanced techniques.

6

Advanced Pixelmator Techniques

In this chapter we will cover some advanced techniques to edit your photos. We will take some real-world examples and cover editing techniques such as colorizing your photos for a vintage effect, creating a black-and-white image, using a tilt-shift effect, and a few more effects.

Using Pixelmator to retouch skin for portrait photography

One very common technique needed for portrait photography is **skin retouching**. Although I am a purist in many ways and don't like retouching to the extent where the final image looks nothing like the original model, there is a need for some slight skin retouching with many portraits. You might have a younger model with pimples that need to be retouched, or someone with a few additional wrinkles that they would like slightly smoothed out in the final portrait. Whatever the case, there are many times where you will need a little skin softening and we will walk through the steps here.

First, start with a portrait image and duplicate the layer. Then open up the **Effects** browser and choose **Gaussian Blur**. Choose a fairly large blur setting; here I am using **35 px** as the radius for the **Gaussian Blur** effect:

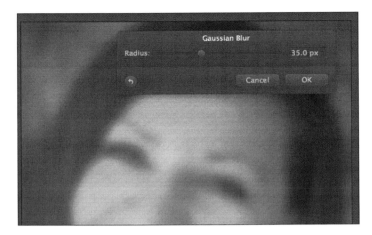

Next, we need to brush out the parts of the photo that we don't want to smooth out. For this, select the eraser tool and choose a soft brush. In the following screenshot, you can see that **Background Layer Copy** is the layer that we applied the blur to and erased the parts we want to remain sharp:

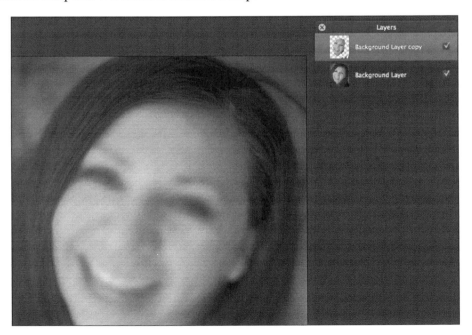

Once you have brushed out the parts and you don't need to soften them further, it's time to fine tune the blur layer more. To get the best view of the layer, which is the blur layer, unselect the main image layer in the layer window. This will now only show the blur layer. You can continue to refine this by using the eraser tool to finish removing any unwanted parts. Also, a good tip for the edges of parts you are erasing is to change the opacity of the eraser tool to be lower, say 40 percent. This will give you a smoother transition. You can see the fine-tuned blur layer in the following screenshot:

Now turn back to the main layer and you will see that the entire face has a blur effect on it. We want certain parts of the face to be in focus, such as the eyes, eyebrows, and mouth. Go back to the blur layer and using the eraser tool again, set the opacity to around 40 percent. Erase the parts of the face that you want to keep in focus, until you get to the point where only the parts of the skin you want to soften are soft and the rest is sharp. Finally, you will want to adjust the opacity of the blur layer to fit your own style and what you feel looks natural and normal. For this example, I set the opacity to **37%** to give a pretty natural feel to the final image:

Softening skin is easy to do and will always help to give your portrait photography a little extra pop by removing the small imperfections of the subject's skin.

Creating a tilt-shift look

Tilt-shift photography has been around for ages, but with the increase in digital photography and ways to create a tilt-shift look in post production, it has been making a comeback. **Tilt-shift photography** refers to the use of camera movements on small- and medium-format cameras, and sometimes specifically refers to the use of tilt for selective focus, often for simulating a miniature scene. Sometimes the term is used when the shallow depth of field is simulated with digital post-processing, but the name does come from the tilt-shift lens normally required when the effect is produced using a camera. Here we will do a tutorial on how to get this look in Pixelmator.

First, it's always best to start with the right image. It will work best if you have an image shot from a high vantage point; so look for an image shot from atop a building or a mountain, looking down. I will always encourage you to try this effect out on many images, so don't feel it's constrained to those types of images; but to first get the feel of how it works, using it on something with a high vantage point can be a good test. Also, images with people, cars, or boats are good to use since it tends to give these a miniaturized look. So let's take a look at how to do this with a shot on a bridge in Venice.

First, we will need to create a gradient that we will use to blur the top and bottom of the image. Open up the gradient panel (by navigating to **View | Show Gradients** or by using the *Command + 5* shortcut). Click on the gear icon and select **New Gradient**. Here, you will want a gradient that has white on both sides and black in the center.

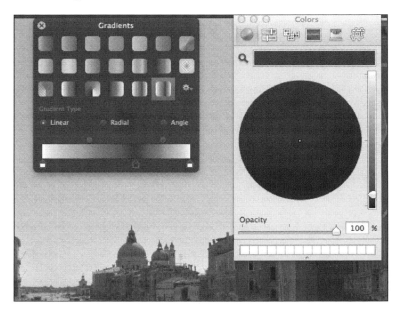

Before you apply the gradient, click on the **Edit in quick mask** mode in the **Edit** menu. This will turn the canvas red to show you the mask you are creating. You will be creating a gradient where the red will be the section of the image that will stay sharp and the non-red parts will be blurry. Click where you would like the transition from blurry to sharp to begin and drag till the point you want it to end. Here I am clicking and dragging from near the top of the buildings to a little way below the boat:

Now turn the quick mask off by unchecking the **Edit in quick mask** option. You will see the mask disappear and be replaced with a selection. Even though it looks like the selection has a sharp edge, it does include the gradient that you made in the earlier step.

Next, open up the **Effects** browser and choose the **Gaussian Blur** option. The radius of the blur depends on the exact image, but normally something in the range of 10 to 20 will work well. In this example, let's use a 13 px blur. After you choose the blur, use the *Command + D* shortcut to remove the selection.

You will notice the edges have a small gradient to them as well. To fix this, just select the blur tool and blur out the edges around all four sides of the image.

The last characteristic that many tilt images have is a heightened saturation and contrast. The first step we will make to modify the colors will be opening up the **Levels** setting. Move the **Black** and **White** points closer to the middle of the histogram to add contrast to the image.

The final step is to bump up the saturation on the image. In the **Effects** window, open up the Hue and Saturation tool and slide the overall saturation up to between 10 percent and 20 percent. That's it; without the high cost of a tilt-shift lens, you have a cool tilt-shift effect on your photo!

Colorizing photos for a vintage look

Vintage looks in photography have been very popular lately; the huge rise in Instagram and other photo filter apps is making it more and more popular. There are many different types of vintage looks you can edit your photo with, but in this chapter we will talk about how to colorize your images to give them a vintage look.

Before we begin to change color levels in Pixelmator, there are eight predefined vintage presets that do have a very nice look to them. The **Vintage** set of filters can be found in the **Effects** panel under the **Stylize** section. When you choose the vintage effect, a screen with more options will appear that gives you the ability to select one of the eight effects and adjust the saturation and vignette of the effects. Take some time to get to know these effects; if you love the vintage look, you will enjoy using these presets. Here is an example using the built-in **Bouvardia** effect:

In this section we are going to cover how to use the **Colorize** option to create a vintage feel.

A very simple way to create a vintage look to your photos is using the built-in **Sepia** effect in the **Color Adjustments** section of the **Effects** panel. This gives you a very basic sepia effect though; if you want more control over the color of the image, select the **Colorize** effect. Here you will see a color wheel that you can spin around to get the exact color you like. Also adjust the saturation and lightness to your liking:

Then add some monochrome noise by checking **Monochrome** on the **Noise** effect dialog box, to give it a little more of an aged feel. In just a few steps, you have a vintage-looking effect.

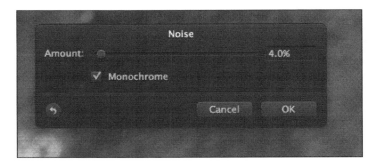

The perfect black-and-white print

Black-and-white photography can have such a beautiful, classic look to it. To begin with, you may tend to use just the **Desaturate** or the **Black and White** effect in the **Color Adjustments** effect panel; however, there are other ways that can give you more control to create the perfect black-and-white print.

Let's walk through creating a black-and-white image. Start with the image you would like to convert to black and white, and add a new layer. Fill this layer with black and change the **Blending** option of this layer to **Color**. Then select the main layer and choose the **Curves** effect. Here you can choose the **Red**, **Green**, and **Blue** colors and adjust each curve to get the exact black-and-white effect, according to your liking:

There is another black-and-white trick you might want to try out. For this one, perform the following steps:

1. Click on the **Desaturate** effect in the **Effects** browser.

2. Next, duplicate the layer and select the **Multiply** blending option. This will give you a very deep black-and-white look, and you can tune down the opacity slider to adjust the effect to as much as you would like:

There are many, many different ways to create a black-and-white image in Pixelmator. Try them all and see what works best for you. Just like anything in the creative process of postproduction, you should take the time to learn all the tools and figure out what works best with your workflow.

Creating an HDR look

High Dynamic Range (**HDR**) is used in photography to enhance detail in the shadows, mid-tones, and highlights. This can be done while shooting the image, by taking multiple exposures and combining them into one image; however, many a times you aren't thinking about HDR while shooting, and later on want to have that HDR look in your photo. We will start with a fairly flat image of the beach and will turn this into a HDR image.

The following is the initial image:

Start by opening up your image and duplicating the background layer twice. Now that you have three layers, go to the very top layer and apply a small Gaussian blur to the layer. For this example, I chose a 2 px Gaussian blur. Then change the layer blending mode to **Soft Light**:

Next, move down to the middle layer and use the **Desaturate** effect. After that, go to the **Light & Dark** effect and move the **Shadows** and **Highlights** to **50%** each. To give a little more color to the image, reduce the opacity of this layer down to about **70%**. Now you have an HDR effect on your image in just a few steps.

Summary

In this chapter we covered a few real-world examples on advanced image editing. You learned how to retouch skin, create a tilt-shift look, and give a vintage feel to your photos. We put many of the primary concepts of Pixelmator that we learned at the start of the book into use. Now that you have a good understanding of how to use Pixelmator to creatively edit your photos, it's time to have some fun and get busy editing. The only thing stopping you now is your own creativity! Have fun and remember to never stop dreaming and creating art.

Index

Contrast blending option 47
cropping 21
crop tool 21
Crystallize effect 66
curves
  adjusting 62
Curves effect 62, 93

D

Darken blending option 47
Desaturate effect 94
Digital single-lens reflex (DSLR) 9, 60
Displacement effect 59
distortion effects
  Bar swipe effect 60
  Bump effect 57
  Capsule effect 59
  Circle splash effect 59
  Circular wrap effect 60
  Displacement effect 59
  Glass effect 60
  Glass ring effect 59
  Hole effect 58
  Linear bump 57
  Page curl effect 58
  Pinch effect 57
  Ripple effect 58
  Twirl effect 60
  Vortex effect 60
  working with 57
Distort option, Transform tool 31
dodging
  about 23
  example 24, 25
dots per inch (DPI) 6
drop shadow
  creating, steps 75

E

Edges effect 67
Edges option 61
Edge Work effect 67
Edit in quick mask mode 88
Elliptical Marquee tool 32
eraser tool 81
Exposure effect 63

F

files
  importing 6-9
fill
  using, for backgrounds 77-79
flipping 31
Fog effect 67

G

Gaussian blur effect 54, 84
Generator effects 67
Glass effect 60
Glass ring effect 59
Gloom effect 67
gradients
  using, for backgrounds 77-79
Gradients toolbar 78
guides 13-16

H

Halftone effects 67
Hatched effect 44
HDR look
  about 94
  creating 94-96
healing tool
  about 71
  using 72
Heal Selection option 72
High Dynamic Range. *See* HDR look
Hole effect 58
Honeycomb effect 66
Hue filter 65

I

images
  burning 23, 24
  color, adjusting 19, 20
  cropping 21
  dodging 23, 24
  editing 18
  enhancing 18

Skew option 30
  working with 30
Transition option 57
Twilight effect 67
Twirl effect 60

U

Unsharp option 61

V

Vintage effect 67
vintage look
  photos, colorizing for 91, 92
Vortex effect 60

W

workspace
  customizing 11

Z

Zoom blur effect 55

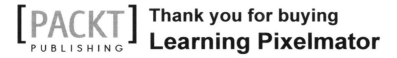

About Packt Publishing

Packt, pronounced 'packed', published its first book "*Mastering phpMyAdmin for Effective MySQL Management*" in April 2004 and subsequently continued to specialize in publishing highly focused books on specific technologies and solutions.

Our books and publications share the experiences of your fellow IT professionals in adapting and customizing today's systems, applications, and frameworks. Our solution based books give you the knowledge and power to customize the software and technologies you're using to get the job done. Packt books are more specific and less general than the IT books you have seen in the past. Our unique business model allows us to bring you more focused information, giving you more of what you need to know, and less of what you don't.

Packt is a modern, yet unique publishing company, which focuses on producing quality, cutting-edge books for communities of developers, administrators, and newbies alike. For more information, please visit our website: www.packtpub.com.

Writing for Packt

We welcome all inquiries from people who are interested in authoring. Book proposals should be sent to author@packtpub.com. If your book idea is still at an early stage and you would like to discuss it first before writing a formal book proposal, contact us; one of our commissioning editors will get in touch with you.

We're not just looking for published authors; if you have strong technical skills but no writing experience, our experienced editors can help you develop a writing career, or simply get some additional reward for your expertise.

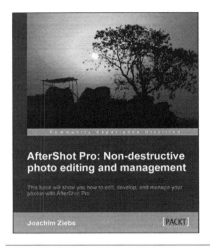

AfterShot Pro: Non-destructive photo editing and management

ISBN: 978-1-849694-66-7   Paperback: 116 pages

This book will show you how to edit, develop, and manage your photos with AfterShot Pro

1. Non-destructively edit your photos

2. Develop your RAW files into stunning images

3. Manage your photos with ease

Sony Vegas Pro 11 Beginner's Guide

ISBN: 978-1-849691-70-3   Paperback: 264 pages

Edit videos with style and ease using Vegas Pro

1. Edit slick, professional videos of all kinds with Sony Vegas Pro

2. Learn audio and video editing from scratch

3. Speed up your editing workflow

4. A practical beginner's guide with a fast-paced but friendly and engaging approach towards video editing

Please check **www.PacktPub.com** for information on our titles

Final Cut Pro X Cookbook

ISBN: 978-1-849692-96-0   Paperback: 452 pages

Edit with style and ease using the latest editing technologies in Final Cut Pro X!

1. Edit slick, professional videos of all kinds – music videos, promos, documentaries, even feature films

2. Add hundreds of built-in animated titles, transitions, and effects without complicated keyframing

3. Learn tons of time-saving workflows to tricky, yet common editing scenarios

4. A guide with a great range of tools for editors of every skill level

Avid Media Composer 6.x Cookbook

ISBN: 978-1-849693-00-4   Paperback: 422 pages

Over 160 highly effective and practical recipes to help beginning and intermediate users get the most from Avid Media Composer 6 editing

1. Hands-on recipes in a step-by-step logical approach to quickly get started with Avid Media Composer and gain deeper understanding

2. Learn Avid Media Composer in a completely new way— gain intensive exposure with various editing options to develop your abilities, become even more creative, and acquaint yourself with various methods that you never thought were possible

Please check **www.PacktPub.com** for information on our titles

33617302R00068

Made in the USA
Lexington, KY
01 July 2014